Research Mistakes

in the Social and Behavioral Sciences

LEROY WOLINS

The Iowa State University Press, Ames

Leroy Wolins is Professor of Psychology and Statistics, Iowa State University, Ames. He received his B.A., M.A., and Ph.D. degrees from Ohio State University.

Printed by
The Iowa State University Press
Ames, Iowa 50010

First edition, 1982

Library of Congress Cataloging in Publication Data

Wolins, Leroy, 1927–
   Research mistakes in the social and behavioral sciences

   Bibliography: p.
   Includes index.
   1. Social sciences—Research. I. Title.
H62.W626   300′.72   82–15285
ISBN 0-8138-0361-6   AACR2

C O N T E N T S

PREFACE

I believe in the validity of Roberts' (1978) statement that "persistent illogic . . . cannot be cured successfully and lastingly by presentation and discussion of horrible misuses of statistics."

Evidence for this generalization is available in many sources. For example, Lewis and Burke (1949) point out some misuse of the chi-square test and the *Psychological Bulletin* devoted over 20 pages to a discussion of this topic in subsequent issues (Good 1968). Yet the same misuse Lewis and Burke discuss as occurring in the psychological literature (Braunstein et. al. 1973, Frieze and Snyder 1980) is still found. Roberts has been in a position to know, for he with W. A. Wallis wrote a textbook in which misapplications were incorporated as part of the material presented (Wallis and Roberts 1956). These misapplications or fallacies were simple and delightful. For example, they report as a regression artifact the observation that outstanding, novice baseball players do less well their second year. However, it may hit the social scientists closer to home if the fallacy occurs with faculty salaries or race differences in intelligence.

Pointing out how statistical fallacies influence public policy will remind the social scientist that good statistics are a necessity, and they need to be reminded. Roberts (1978) implies the typical users of statistics need a "cook book"—they do not understand statistics and paranoia prevails. The academic social science departments want fewer and easier statistics and of course others feel they need more statistics (Pieters 1976) that are better taught (Kempthorne 1980). It seems that the statistical consultant, like Moses, is perceived with a

mixture of awe and antipathy. Too often he appears to
disallow the obvious and to recommend the incomprehensible
(Bross 1974, Marquardt 1979).

Statistics is essential to the social sciences and we
need the cooperation of these scientists to improve our
teaching of statistics. What needs to be done, in my
opinion, is to offer a constant barrage of statistical
criticism to the social science literature. We should attend to misuses in the context of important issues on either theoretical or socially relevant topics. We should
criticize frequently cited journal articles appropriately
and ignore misuse of statistics in obtuse contexts. The
latter would excite only the author who should appreciate
a letter of explanation, but in my experience does not.
Authors often respond defensively and sometimes cite textbooks that have either carelessly or inaccurately applied
the procedure used by authors of these journal articles.
It is better to voice publicly one's criticism. Some substantial investment of journal pages to statistical and
methodological mistakes, and the controversies that would
ensue, has the potential of saving money and advancing
the social-behavioral sciences.

Thus the statement by Roberts (1978) could be amended
to some advantage. It is possible that well-defined persistent illogic *can* be ameliorated for a *short time* by
presentation and discussion of horrible misuses of statistics. A short term remission for a well-defined class
of statistical misuses could be valuable since the cost of
research is high--even a masters thesis is expensive.

An economic perspective on research is obviously appropriate. Whether the problem is defined by a graduate
student or an executive committee of a large corporation,
there are economic constraints, anticipated benefits, and
risks. This book deals with the risk that money invested
in obtaining information through data collection and analysis is lost because of illogic and misuse of statistics.

There seems to be an infinite number of ways to misuse statistics. Perusal or an appropriate body of literature will reveal to the sophisticated statistician a tre-
mendous variety of statistical misuses.

Discussion of isolated misuses can be valuable from
the point of view of research questions, but to the peda-
gogy of statistics it can be valuable only to the extent
that it is illustrative of a broad class of misuses. I
have accrued a large assortment of statistical misuses
over the years and find that certain ones recur and fit

into broad classes. The basis for a class is a particular illogic. I have attempted to deal with the illogic and to use the particular misuses to illustrate the illogic and to convince the reader of the importance of the illogic.

Most misuses I have found do not fit into these broad classes and many of those that fit into one class fit other classes as well. Thus the classes are neither mutually exclusive nor exhaustive. Yet this structure I have imposes may be sufficiently orderly so that the readers may carry away some circumscribed concepts that will enhance their ability to be critical.

Since the organization of the book is based on classifying misuses, no attempt has been made to proceed from simple to complex or to integrate one chapter with another. I have attempted to reify these classes so that their names have meaning in the context in which they are presented and can be used for succinct criticism.

Since the complexity of the material is highly variable, a person with a few courses in statistics cannot be expected to comprehend all of this book. Thus my audience is necessarily restricted to those with substantial knowledge of statistical methods and psychological measurement.

Interspersed throughout the text are tangential, usually technical comments. They are essential to the main idea but break the continuity. Readers may skip over them but should return to them and familiarize themselves with their context. They are placed where I feel they make sense in context.

My strategy for citing references is conservative. Other things being equal, I cite references to recently published articles. If a mistake appears so prevalent as to be common practice in my judgment (e.g., reporting significance levels for regression coefficients derived for a reduced model), I cite few or no references. If I feel the reader may doubt the extensiveness of the mistake, I cite as many references as I can find.

Finally, this book is not intended to be a general criticism of research in the social-behavioral sciences. To find a misuse worthy of comment I must peruse many journal articles. Most of what I read is well done in all respects and I sense notable improvement in our research efforts over the years. My motivations for writing this book, as well as my previous writings, are open to criticism and undoubtedly I will be appropriately criticized. When I am, I will feel badly; yet I would feel worse if I

were ignored and my mistakes went uncorrected. Perhaps
all I can do is to hope that my audience is similarly mo-
tivated in this delicate area.

I wish to acknowledge my indebtedness to my teacher,
R. J. Wherry. I learned much from him. I also learned
from my colleagues in statistics at Iowa State University,
past and present, as well as staff and visitors who
through seminars and casual conversation shared their ideas. I listened to these colleagues and they listened to
me. Finally, I am grateful to Robert F. Boruch, who en-
ticed me into this project and arranged financial support
through NIE-G-79-0128 and NSF Grant DAR-7820374, which
gave me six months to spend in the library and to think
and to write.

REFERENCES

Braunstein, D. N., G. A. Klein, and M. Pachla. 1973.
    Feedback expectancy and shifts in student ratings of
    college faculty. *Journal of Applied Psychology*, pp.
    254-58.
Bross, I. D. J. 1974. The role of the statistician:
    Scientist or shoe clerk. *American Statistician*, pp.
    126-27.
Frieze, I. H., and H. N. Snyder. 1980. Children's be-
    liefs about the causes of success and failure in
    school settings. *Journal of Educational Psychology*,
    pp. 186-96.
Good, I. J. 1968. Statistical Fallacies. *International
    Encyclopedia of the Social Sciences*, vol. 5, pp. 292-
    301. New York: Macmillan and Free Press.
Kempthorne, O. 1980. The teaching of statistics: Con-
    tent versus form. *American Statistician*, pp. 17-21.
Lewis, D., and C. J. Burke. 1949. The use and misuse of
    the chi-square test. *Psychological Bulletin*, pp.
    433-89.
Marquardt, D. W. 1979. Statistical consulting in indus-
    try. *American Statistician*, pp. 102-7.
Pieters, R. S. 1976. Statistics in the high school cur-
    riculum. *American Statistician*, pp. 134-39.
Roberts, H. V. 1978. Statisticians can matter. *American
    Statistician*, pp. 45-51.
Wallis, W. A., and H. V. Roberts. 1956. *Statistics: A
    New Approach*. New York: Free Press.

RESEARCH MISTAKES

1

Power, Sufficiency, Admissability Problems

The purpose of this chapter on the Power, Sufficiency, Admissability Problem (PSAP) is to impress the reader with the importance of money in designing research and analyzing data. Generally speaking, the purpose of research is to obtain information. Like any other enterprise we wish to optimize and we wish to design research and analyze the results to obtain the most information for the dollar.

This does not imply that each researcher is obligated to extract all the information that is in the data. For example, an interpretation of Tyler's (1978) discussion would encourage experimental psychologists to compare error terms in repeated measurement designs because such comparisons are of interest to differential psychologists but are ancillary to the interests of the experimental psychologists. Here we are concerned with studies directed at a particular question and inefficiencies in design and analysis related to that particular question and not to other questions for which the data may be relevant. It is inconsiderate to neglect the interests of others when it is easy to cater to them, but that is not the issue being addressed here. Nor are the power problems that Cohen (1962) has treated of particular concern. There is little one could add to that impressive work.

For a better definition of the topic consider the three data sets in Table 1.1. Consider that eight scores in each data set are obtained from measuring four people twice: before a treatment (T_1) and after a treatment (T_2). Further, consider that the actual measurement procedure resulted in scores that did not behave nicely so

Table 1.1. Three data sets; *A*, *B* and *C*; involving two treatments and four observational units

	A		B		C	
	T_1	T_2	T_1	T_2	T_1	T_2
1)	1	2	1	5	1	8
2)	3	4	2	6	2	7
3)	5	6	3	7	3	6
4)	7	8	4	8	4	5

that only the rank of the eight scores are reported. For example, these eight scores could come from four autistic children measured with (T_1) and without (T_2) a medicine.

The measure might be obtained from video tapes of the children in a controlled setting and judges who evaluate time segments of these tapes according to the amount of time the children attend to external sources of stimulation as contrasted with children that are being completely withdrawn and ignore a changing environment. Keep in mind that the original measures are available even though only the rank ordering is reported.

Look at these data sets without any statistical analysis. Data set *B* appears to be the ideal outcome--the worst child under medication is better than the best without. A sample of four is small for normative purposes. But it seems intuitively obvious that this outcome is better than the one for data set *A*, since there no child surpasses an adjacentally scoring one because of the treatment. The outcomes for both data sets *A* and *B* are similar in that the rank ordering of the children remains the same under the two treatments. This is appealing since the facts of life seem to indicate behavior is consistent when reliably measured. Even with normal children one would expect consistent behavior over time if the measurement were reliable.

Data set *C*, like *B*, indicates the worst child under medication is better than the best without. But the child who was worst off was helped most by the medication and the most alert prior to medication appears to have been helped the least. This would upset one's expectations and detract from the credibility of the findings. These results suggest that either the medication varies in effectiveness or the measurement procedure is unreliable.

The normative information available from these ranks is not *qualitatively* different from the information obtained from well-developed measurement processes. Standardized tests, for example, are based on large, representative samples and thereby the information is better but

it is not different. The greater belief in the treatment
effects derived from the B results is based on the more
likely occurrence of high concordance when individual differences are large. *If* individual differences are large,
one should be impressed that the worst child when medicated is better than the best when not medicated. Similarly,
for the C results, apparent negative concordance is more
likely to occur when individual differences are small so
that the lack of overlap of the ranks under the two treatment conditions is less impressive.

There are other considerations in evaluating the degree of concordance. The precision of measurement will
also influence the degree of concordance so that one must
believe the measurement procedure is equally precise for
the B and C results in order to compare them. Diurnal or
temporal variability also tends to lower concordance.
Subject by treatment interaction could produce the C results, but it is appropriate that such interaction should
detract from the credibility of the treatment effects.

If one had a standardized and reliable measure that
was based on a large number of autistic children, one
would be able to compare directly the magnitude of the individual differences and the magnitude of the changes from
different studies if the individual differences occurred
over the same part of the scale. For example, if one subject changed from the fiftieth percentile to the sixtieth
percentile and another changed from the fiftieth percentile to the seventieth percentile, one should attribute
greater magnitude to the latter change. However, comparing a change from 40 to 50 on some scale with a change
from 50 to 60 on that same scale could be appropriate if
one had considerable data regarding the *change* produced by
the treatment. One might construct a scale based on these
data in a way that the changes are additive over the range
of the scale. If one could do that, the changes could be
compared in the same normative sense as the scores. One
would be comparing an individual's change with the other
individuals' changes who had similar scores to the single
individual under no-treatment or control conditions. Later discussion in this book deals more extensively with
evaluating magnitudes.

Given this look at the data, we next search for a
probability basis for our inferences. How do we analyze
such data? I use a book by Ott (1977) in a course I
teach, so what does he say? He states in his chapter on
"Nonparametric Methods" that, "some studies yield data

identified by rank only. . . ." Thus I'm in the right
chapter and the first thing I find is the Sign Test, which
is for paired data. I read it and find I can use it. But
if I do, I get the same answer for all three of the data
sets, which doesn't seem right; so I read on and find Wilcoxon's Signed-Rank Test, "which makes use of the sign and
the magnitude of the rank of the differences between pairs
of measurements. . . ." Make use of the magnitude? What
happened here? I thought we were talking about "data
identified by rank only. . . ." Oh well, I am glad I read
it carefully because I only want to use the ordinal information and not magnitudes of differences occurring at different places on my messy scale. So I read on and find
Wilcoxon's Rank Sum Test, which some people call the Mann-
Whitney U test. But I find I can't use it because that
test is for comparing two populations and I have a sample
from only one population. I read on and find nothing relevant, so I go to Snedecor and Cochran (1967), Ostle and
Mensing (1975), and others (Ferguson 1971; Steel and
Torrie 1960; Bradley 1968) and find much the same discussion, except these other books do not mention that the
signed-rank test ranks magnitudes. Maybe that is not important. I look further and I find Blalock (1979) and
Conover (1971), and indeed the assumptions stated in both
books include the interval measurement one, so I am left
with the sign test. Right? Wrong!

Why can't I use the rank-sum test for these data? It
is a permutation test that tells me out of all 8! permuta-
tions only $(4!)^2$ of them would give me results as extreme
as data sets B and C. Also, the rank-sum test indicates
the results are significant, whereas the sign test indicates $p > .05$. There is no reason for failing to use this
rank-sum test. It uses information in the data without
using information that is not in the data.

But what about the difference between data set B and
C? Certainly one should be more comfortable with the B
results than the C results, but the rank-sum test gives
the same result for both of these data sets. I looked
further and found one cannot incorporate this feeling into
a nonparametric statistic requiring only ordinal information. One should teach his students that there is a concept of nonadditivity that pertains to ordinal data.

But what about situation A? The probability derived
from the sign test is 1/16 and the rank-sum test gives an
even larger probability. Yet the fact that $T_1 > T_2$ for

all four observations and the rank ordering of the four observations is the same for both treatments seems to provide even more compelling evidence against H_0 than situation C in which the rank ordering resulting from the two treatments are opposite to what one should expect.

I also note, temerariously, that the t-test results in a very small p-value for situations A and B but not for situation C.

Apropos the autistic children, it seems that the three results should invite three different inferences. Situation A suggests the medicine is effective but more data is needed before implementation. Situation B indicates the medicine is effective and one should start implementation on some limited scale. Situation C suggests that the medicine helps those who are badly off in the first place but is of doubtful use for the less severely introverted.

These inferences are not based exclusively on any one of these statistical tests. Although the probability bases for these inferences are available from these statistics, they are vague; they either use information not in the data or ignore relevant information. There is no good way to come up with a single number to indicate our faith in the results. In making these three inferences I have resorted to intuition, the other vagueness, which could be considered the lesser evil, but that is not the main point. The main point is that authors of textbooks owe it to their audiences to point out this particular vagueness; namely, there is no right way to analyze statistically paired observations using only ordinal information.

You should ask, Why have I make this point in this context since it is almost always true that statistical summarizations do not use all the information in data? I answer that in other situations the information loss is due to failure to meet assumptions but in this case it is not possible to design a statistical test that uses the block information in which the treatments are compared. That is, in situations A and B the concordance is high but the sign test gives the same answer, and in situation C the concordance is low but again we get the same answer. If one used the t-test, situation C is identified as different from the other two and situations A and B are distinguished because the treatments are estimable in the context of the assumptions. Thus the sign test and the rank-sum test may loose some information because they *can not* use it, whereas such information is useable for other significance tests, but there is usually some loss because of failure to meet assumptions.

These problems are frequently noted in the current literature. Wilcoxon's signed-rank test is used for the wrong reason (Dunleary and Baade 1980; Durlach and Rescorla 1980; Knudson et. al. 1980; Lewis and Maurer 1979) and less often the sign test is used when the scores are completely ordered (Foa et. al. 1980).

Before leaving this area of nonparametric analysis consider the following statement from Siegel (1956) after a Komologorov-Smirnov two-sample test: "We conclude that eleventh-graders make proportionally fewer errors than seventh-graders in recalling the first half of a learned series." Recall that this test statistic is somewhat sensitive to all of the many ways that these two distributions may differ yet Siegel makes a location inference. Siegel did not defend this position, so I will.

Imagine a density distribution of some form--normal if you wish--sitting on a line where the intervals are labeled 1, 2, 3, etc., but instead of being equally spaced, the intervals are spaced unequally and unsystematically. Now change the location of the distribution. What changes? Everything changes! All the moments carry information about this change in location. Of course it is risky to use this test statistic because it could be significant even when no change in location occurred. But Siegel presents the raw data and the change in location is apparent. So it is the presentation of the data and its inspection that makes the inference defensible. Again we see the notion of sufficiency is not germane because of the messy, ad hoc scales used in the social sciences. Conover (1971) has a nice presentation of this problem, but this brings us to the illogic of the typical presentation in textbooks of the Behrens-Fisher problem.

This illogic is that they recommend a preliminary test to see if the variances are equal. If they are not equal, according to this preliminary test, they recommend a conservative test for location. But if the intervals are unequal, and I argue in Chapter 3 that we can never claim they are equal, the variances carry information about location. Thus in a stepwise fashion one is invited to discard information that may be relevant to the question to which the research is directed. Again the probability bases for the inference are present but there is no way they can be sufficient--one must peruse the data. The orthodoxy of certain journal editors in this regard has been frustrating to many good scientists and the literature abounds in these kinds of mistakes.

The Behrens-Fisher problem becomes serious, according to these textbooks, if the sample sizes are small and unequal; so it follows, according to a further illogic, that one should allocate OUs to treatments equally. To appreciate this illogic one must contemplate carefully the difference between a situation in which the researcher has control of the sample sizes and one in which he takes what he can get. *In the former case there is no problem.* In textbooks in survey sampling we are told correctly that the larger sample size should go to the group with the larger variance and techniques are described which tell you precisely how to allocate sample sizes when the variances are known and unequal. It seems strange that no such discussion occurs in methods books or books in experimental design. Certainly in many areas we know beforehand that certain kinds of treatments or groups result in more variability than others. For example, automated instruction usually results in less variability in achievement than classical classroom procedures, women respond more variably to attitude questions than men, and whites are more variable in IQ than blacks. One can use such information in planning research and should be encouraged to do so rather than discouraged by admonitions to keep the sample sizes equal.

On the other hand, if sample sizes are not under the control of the researcher the Behrens-Fisher problem is a problem but it is only then that the typical admonitions of these textbook writers are correct. If one knows beforehand that the variances are unequal, it is wrong to allocate equal sample sizes. Most often we do not know precisely what the variances are, but an intelligent guess will probably result in more power than blindly allocating equally.

Cost of treatment is another aspect of research planning that is regularly ignored. It is extremely common to find research reports in the experimental literature comparing two or more treatments varying widely in cost yet sample sizes used are equal across treatment groups. Again, textbooks in survey sampling handle this topic carefully but, as far as I know, it does not occur in methods books or in intermediate level books on experimental design. Moreover, one obtains greater power from allocating the larger sample to the less expensive treatment, and an intelligent guess at relative costs should result in more power than equal allocation of observational units.

Another aspect of the Behrens-Fisher problem, not attended to but should be, is its complete relevance only when two populations are being compared rather than when two treatments are being compared. Under null conditions, *no* treatment effects, the variances must be equal. If the variances are unequal, there must be a treatment effect. Of course the treatment might effect the variance but not the mean, the mean but not the variance, or both the mean and the variance. But these are nonnull conditions and the test statistic makes no promises about nonnull distributions. Thus test statistics are all right even when the sample sizes are small and unequal and when the variances are unequal. Naturally we are concerned with nonnull distributions, but we should make clear both where and when there is a Behrens-Fisher problem. If the research is truly experimental with randomization, etc., the test for equal variances and the test for equal means are theoretically independent assessments of a null hypothesis or, if you wish, null hypotheses.

SUMMARY

Somewhere along the line social scientists have been led to believe that summary statistics, particularly tests of significance, can convey the information in data completely. Fads and fashions have dominated logic. Pure statistical thinking has led us away from data. In many cases, particularly when one is working in a well established area in which the procedures and measures are standardized, it really isn't fair to look at that data in order to decide how to analyze it. But most of the literature I read does not fit that description. It is exploratory, and looking at the data is by far the lesser evil. Data contains information and unless you know where that information lies (e.g. in the location parameters or elsewhere) you will probably do a better job of retrieving it by inspection than by routine application of test statistics.

What one must do is to plan research carefully. Think about the data before you collect it. Ask yourself what information is needed and make cost estimates of the various ways such information may be obtained. For each potential data collection procedure try to imagine the many possible outcomes. For each of these you can imagine, plan how the data may be analyzed and communicated to an audience. Seek out the opinions of colleagues. Show them potential outcomes you envision and ask them to interpret the results. If they find the results ambiguous, probe to find out what kind of information they would seek.

Finally, the Behrens-Fisher problem is surrounded by confusion. In a true experiment in the behavioral-social sciences, the variances cannot be unequal under null conditions because if they are unequal it must be caused by the treatment. It is possible that only the variances are altered by the treatments but in my judgment that possibility is so small that it can be neglected. Thus even when the experimenter observes unequal variances, he should proceed in the usual manner rather than resorting to conservative tests based on approximate distributions because he knows that truly null conditions will result in identical distributions for the two treatments. The only thing that statistical tables promise is that the probability under null conditions is accurate. There are other factors that can disturb these null distributions beside the Behrens-Fisher problem, but the solution to these problems are generally nonparametric statistics.

REFERENCES
Blalock, H. M., Jr. 1979. *Social Statistics*. 2d ed., rev. New York: McGraw-Hill.
Bradley, James V. 1968. *Distribution-free Statistical Tests*. Englewood Cliffs, N. J.: Prentice-Hall.
Cohen, J. 1962. The statistical power of abnormal-social psychological research: A review. *Journal of abnormal and Social Psychology*, pp. 145-53.
Conover, W. J. 1971. *Practical Nonparametric Statistics*. Wiley: New York.
Dunleary, R. A., and L. E. Baade. 1980. Neuropsychological correlates of severe asthma in children 9-14 years old. *Journal of Consulting and Clinical Psychology*, pp. 214-19.
Durlach, P. J., and R. A. Rescorla. 1980. Potentiation rather than overshadowing in flavor-aversion learning: An analysis in terms of within-compound associations. *Journal of Experimental Psychology. Animal Behavior Processes*, pp. 175-87.
Ferguson, G. A. 1971. *Statistical Analysis in Psychology and Education*. 3d. ed. New York: McGraw-Hill.

Foa, E. G., G. Stekettee, and J. B. Milby. 1980. Differ-
    ential Effects of Exposure and Response Prevention in
    Obsessive-Compulsive Washers. *Journal of Consulting
    and Clinical Psychology*, pp. 71-79.
Knudson, R. M., A. A. Sommers, and S. L. Golding. 1980.
    Interpersonal perception and mode of resolution in
    marital conflict. *Journal of Personality and Social
    Psychology*, pp. 751-63.
Lewis, T. L., and D. Maurer. 1979. Central vision in the
    newborn, *Journal of Experimental Child Psychology*,
    pp. 475-80.
Ostle, B., and R. W. Mensing. 1975. *Statistics in Re-
    search*. 3d ed. Ames: Iowa State University.
Ott, L. 1977. *An Introduction to Statistical Methods and
    Data Analysis*. North Scituate, Mass.: Duxbury
    Press.
Siegel, S. 1956. *Nonparametric Statistics for the Behav-
    ioral Sciences*. New York: McGraw-Hill.
Snedecor, G. W., and W. G. Cochran. 1967. *Statistical
    Methods*. 6th ed. Ames: Iowa State University
    Press.
Steel, R. G., and J. H. Torrie. 1960. *Principles and
    Procedures of Statistics*. New York: McGraw-Hill.
Tyler, L. E. 1978. *Individuality*. San Francisco:
    Jossey-Bass.

2

Regression Toward the Mean Mistake

In my opinion Regression Toward the Mean Mistake (RTMM) is the most persistent, complex, and insidious of all mistakes. I confronted it for the first time as a graduate student and it is promoted (Wildt and Ahtola 1978) as well as damned (Woodward and Goldstein 1977) in many different forms right up to the present. Lord (1967) describes it in its simple form and many studies illustrate it with real data.

In its simple form this mistake involves individuals in two or more treatment groups who are measured twice. The first measure is obtained before treatment, and the second—identical to the first—is obtained after treatment. The question the procedure is intended to answer is, Do the groups differ on the second measure when group differences on the first measure are taken into account?

If the groups do not differ on the first measure or such differences occur only by chance, the usual procedures for adjustment may be beneficial because it may reduce the error variance. If the groups do differ on the former measure, some absurd assumptions must be met before the results can be interpreted in a straightforward manner. These assumptions include the usual ones plus the assumption that the former measure is error free and reflects only what it is intended to measure. For example, it is necessary to assume that control variables are free of method variance as defined by Campbell and Fiske (1959).

Although the assumption of infallible control variables is the major concern when groups differ on covariates, the usual assumptions warrant careful consideration in all contexts. These may be considered in the context of the usual analysis of covariance model.

Consider the following outline for the interpretation of the assumptions contained in this model:

I. Independence (Determined by the procedure used to select observational units and to treat Observational Units (OUs).)
   A. Randomness
      1. An experimental design enabling one to generalize results to some population: Select randomly from a large population a sample of size n and assign these units to one treatment, select another sample of size n from that population and assign these units to the next treatment, etc.
      2. An experimental design enabling one to make statements about a single sample, rather than a population, where either it is not expected that properties of the OUs would influence the results or an expedient that is necessary because a random sample is not available: Select some OUs, not necessarily randomly. Randomly partition these units into as many equal (or nearly equal) size groups as there are treatments. Assign one group to each treatment.
      3. (An investigation—*not* an experiment.) Select randomly from one population a sample of size n. Select randomly from some *other* population a sample of size n, etc.
      4. (For lack of a better name, we call this a study.) Take the OUs available or at hand to represent one population, take the OUs at hand to represent some other population, etc. When this design is used, the assumption of independence may not be reasonable but the results may be informative if other assumptions are met. That is, if many studies are done and uniform results are obtained, the inference has some support.
   B. Independent handling of OUs.
      1. Treat each OU independently. Do *not* treat units in the same treatment as a

group. Do not allow the OUs within one treatment to interact or influence each other.
2. Do not allow any factor extraneous to the treatment to influence the OUs in any treatment group unless this outside factor is explicitly recognized as part of the treatment.
3. The measurement which takes place following treatment must be handled in a fashion analogous to the treatment. That is, each OU should be measured the same way, and the group an OU is in should not be allowed to influence the measurement procedure.

II. Additivity (Determined by differential treatment effects on observational units or by the scale on which the variate or covariate is measured.)
   A. Homoscedasticity: The variability of OUs on the variate Y in one treatment *and* at one level of the covariate should be the same for all combinations of treatments and levels of the covariate.
   B. Shape characteristics other than variance: Whatever form the distribution of OUs takes on the variate Y in one treatment *and* at one level of the covariate, this form should be the same for all treatments--levels of the covariate combinations.
   C. Linearity: Within each treatment group (or sample from one population) the form of the relationship between X and Y must be linear. Another way of saying this is that a change in X of a given size implies a change in Y of some size, and the size of that change in Y should not depend on *where* the change in X occurs.
   D. Equal slope: The slope of the line that relates X to Y in any one treatment group should be the same as the slope of the line that relates X to Y in any other treatment group.

III. Normality (Determined by the shape of the distribution for the population or by the measurement scale.) The shape of the distribution of the variate Y for each combination of the treatments and levels of the covariate should be normal.

IV. Unbiasedness (Given independence, defined above, the only remaining source of bias is the measurement procedure.) For each combination of the treatment and level of the covariate, the average error is zero.

DISCUSSION OF THE MODEL

It is fortunate for all concerned that the statistician is a scientist rather than a mathematician. To be sure, statisticians derived the computational formulas and the associated distributions from the assumptions of mathematicians, but they didn't stop with this. They ask next, What happens if one or more assumptions are not met in certain specified ways? For example, What if the distributions are skewed rather than symmetrical? or What if the X variable is measured with some degree of imprecision? etc. To the extent that an assumption used to derive a procedure can be violated, the statistic is *robust* against that assumption. Analysis Of Covariance (ANOCO) is robust against certain of these assumptions under certain conditions (Antigullah 1964, Hamilton 1976, Hamilton 1977) but may be a completely useless and misleading method if other assumptions are violated. The following discussion considers the conditions under which certain assumptions can and cannot be violated.

Independence

Of the four basic assumptions, the most stringent one is the first, independence. It appears to be the least understood and most often violated. It can be violated in two ways, as indicated in the outline; by the way the sample is selected and by the way the observations are treated. Next, two studies are outlined to illustrate each of these violations.

Study 1. Several years ago Iowa State University established a program of study (the Honors Program) enabling talented students to have more freedom in their choices of courses and an opportunity to enroll in special sections of courses. To be eligible for the program, these students must have demonstrated high scholastic achievement and must maintain this high achievement in order to stay in the program. Although the program is available to many students, not all eligible students choose to enroll in it.

In a follow-up study of students in general it was decided to expend special effort to evaluate this program. To do this students who had graduated from this program several years ago were paired with students not enrolled in the program on the basis of grade point average, curriculum, sex, and year of graduation. A stratified random sample was used to select students in general, but all students graduating from the Honors Program and their non-Honors Program counterparts were selected for this study.

In analyzing the results pertinent to evaluating the Honors Program, one must consider the sample size to be, say, 100 pairs rather than 200 people. Also the relevant data for analysis are complete pairs. Thus if 70 of the 100 honors students return their questionnaires, 50 of the 100 matched students return their questionnaires and 40 matched-pairs result; hence the analysis would be based on these 40 observations and the percentage returns would be 40 percent, not 60 percent.

A straightforward example of this kind of mistake occurs in an article by Edelson and Seidman (1975).

Study 2. Nonindependence derived from how the OUs are treated.

This mistake is illustrated in an article by Button (1974) and many other educational research articles. At least some of the time, a teacher will address the whole class. The quality of such presentation will influence everybody in the class, and this quality will not be precisely the same from one presentation to the next. Also the students in classrooms influence each other. One rowdy, obstreperous child makes it difficult for everyone. Several actively participating and inquiring children in a class would enhance the educational experience for everyone, including the teacher, who would enjoy the class more and probably do a better job of teaching because of these children. Thus for purposes of statistical analysis, one should not analyze individuals within classrooms as if they were independent observations. Rather, educators should recognize that the teacher and students are part of a single interacting, dynamic situation and only one statistic can be independently derived.

Further violation of the independence assumption would occur if the same teacher taught several classrooms. Using various measures of teacher effectiveness it is

clear that some teachers are better than others. Consequently each classroom in an experiment should have a different teacher randomly assigned. Other designs are possible in which a teacher instructs several classrooms and
teacher differences are controlled. But such designs are
risky in that the experiences of a teacher with one classroom may influence that teacher's performance in other
classrooms.

Additivity

The independence assumption is of vital importance in
all situations, but the importance of the additivity assumption is much greater for a study or investigation than
it is for an experiment. In an experiment observations
occur in groups randomly and the value for each observation on the covariate is determined prior to treatment.
As a result no differences between groups on the covariate
are *expected* to occur. Of course they will occur, occa-
sionally. Yet because of these *expectations*, rather than
the actual outcome of an experiment, the test statistic
for the covariate is a legitimate test despite moderate
deviations from the additivity assumptions. Moderate, in
this context, is one of those terms that defy precise definition. In most cases one need not concern oneself with
nonadditivity in the context of an experiment in which the
results of the test are interpreted per se. The larger
problem is a potential failure to recognize the treatments
influence observations in ways that produce differences
other than differences between means. Unequal slopes
should not always be viewed as a nuisance, interfering
with the location test, but sometimes as a substantive
finding.

In studies and investigations the additivity assumption may be crucial. This is true since there is no reason to believe that the two groups are the same with respect to the covariate. Actually covariance is sometimes
the method of choice because this method purports to control for group differences on the covariate that might influence the variate. Furthermore, a common misconception
is that the only purpose covariance serves is to adjust
for group differences in such investigations or studies
(Kirk 1968). I hope to convince the reader that ANOCO in
the social sciences is a viable technique only for reducing error. I have never seen it used appropriately for
adjusting for group differences and I cannot imagine a
social science investigation in which covariance could be

legitimately applied for that purpose, although I have
seen many studies in which covariance was used for that
purpose.

The effective use of transformations should result in
closer approximations to all of the additivity requirements. However, it is not uncommon to find that the
transformation that results in more nearly equal variances, also results in greater nonlinearity or unequal
slope. When this happens, transformation on both X and Y
may bring about the best results.

Normality

Given additivity, the normality assumption is seldom
important; if it doesn't occur, there is nothing that can
be done. One hopes that appropriately applied transformations will result in normality as well as additivity. As
before, inspection of the data through scatterplots provides the best basis for judging how well the normality
assumption is met. This inspection should detect extreme
skewness or bimodality, which would preclude the use of
the covariance procedure.

Before leaving these assumptions the reader should
note the *order* in which these assumptions were discussed.
If normality were discussed prior to additivity, one would
be tempted to ignore II.B in the outline. However, if the
shape of a distribution is preserved when the location
changes, then all the information on level or treatment
differences is contained in the location parameter. As a
result the power of the test is enhanced. Lack of normality of the extent typically encountered in social science research is not likely to influence the power of a
test adversely. Thus this additivity requirement is more
important than normality.

More Complex Examples

A more complex variation of RTMM involves a control
measure different from the dependent one. A good example
of this is a report by Bruvold.

The questions Bruvold (1973) deals with are topical
in social psychology: Do both behavior and beliefs influence attitude? The structure of the data here differs
from the previous example in that there are not groups per
se. Rather, three scores are involved. The dependent
variable is the attitude toward a particular swimming
pool. This attitude is measured by a 26-item Thurstone
scale. Each of the other two variables is derived from

the composite of three dichotomous items. Given this, one could construct four groups from either of the two independent variables and thereby manufacture a data structure similar in all respects except that the control variable is different from the dependent one.

Constructing four groups from one of the independent variables is identical to fitting a third order polynomial to the data (Cohen and Cohen 1975). Bruvold fit only the linear, which is not unreasonable. We point this out because the mistake Bruvold makes is not different from the analysis of covariance mistakes previously referred to: the partial correlation or partial regression analysis and associated significance test are fallible in identically the same way as is the test for group differences, given a correlated, fallibly measured control variable. Campbell and Erlbacher (1970) discuss this mistake in this context at some length.

Cohen and Cohen (1975) describe and give examples of this fact. It matters not at all if a degree of freedom is used by specifying two groups or the linear component of a continuous variable. For example, one may analyze age by classifying individuals into three groups; young, middle age, and old. Alternatively, with the same two degrees of freedom, one may use age and age-squared as variables. The latter is to be preferred for hypothesis testing purposes because if age is predictive of the dependent variable, the variability within a class also would be somewhat predictive. The variability within a class is lost when one classifies but is potentially useable by fitting the linear and quadratic. In my experience a quadratic often provides a sufficient fit for social and behavioral science data but sometimes higher order polynomials are required.

Rather than using age (A) and age-squared (A^2) it is better to use A and $(A - \bar{A})^2$ where $\bar{A}$ is the mean age. The reason is that these two variables will be less highly correlated in the latter case and it is less probable that one will be misled by a likely outcome that the test for the partial regression coefficient for neither A nor A^2 is significant because of this high correlation, although either one alone is significantly related to Y. This happens (Mosteller and Tukey 1977).

This recommendation also applies to behavioral science data. A psychologist might observe behavior on each of 60 trials. He may do the analysis using a composite based on 3 trial blocks by summing the measures of the

Table 2.1. Intercorrelations among variables used by Bruvold (1973)

	F	R	E
Belief (F)		.11	.28
Behavior (R)			.30
Attitude (E)			

responses over the first 20, middle 20, and last 20 trials. Even when the behavior is dichotomously scored on
each trial, one expects a reasonably well-behaved variable
from the average over 20 observations. But even when the
responses are scored dichotomously one can probably do
better with the same appeal to the central limit theorem
by analyzing the regression coefficients resulting from
regressing each vector of "0" and "1" numbers on the orthogonal polynomials for 60 trials.

After the test for significance one should resort to
age groups or trial blocks for description or inspection
of the data since polynomial fits are too sensitive to ab-
errant observations, especially in the extremes.

Bruvold (1973) reports the correlations among the
three measures in Table 2.1. The partial regression coefficients for both F and R are statistically significant
leading to the inference that both are relevant for attitude formation. Although the data are consistent with
this interpretation, it is also evident that the 26-item
attitude measure is relatively reliable whereas the 3-item
measures are quite unreliable. The author implies this
conclusion by his statement that the items in the behavior
and belief measures are independent or nearly so.

If one had 32 items altogether where the items correlate .04 on the average, and one randomly assigned the
items to three scales of size 3, 3 and 26, respectively,
one would obtain results very similar to those of Bruvold.
Thus Bruvold's inference is not necessarily supported by
the data. It may be that all three scales fallibly reflect the same trait, and the prediction of attitude by
both belief and behavior is due to both measures resulting
in a more reliable measure of the pervasive trait than either one alone.

The mistake crops up in context of studies of race
differences. For example, government regulations demand
that tests and other devices used for job selection be
equally valid for blacks and whites. This might be trans-
lated operationally to the two groups having the same intercept and slope. Slope differences can occur because of
unequal scale intervals, which is discussed in Chapter 3.
But measurement error is always expected to produce

intercept differences, which should not be interpreted as
evidence that the test is functioning differently for
blacks and whites. These intercept differences may merely
indicate that the measure is fallible and whites regress
to the mean of whites on the criterion whereas blacks regress to the mean of blacks on the criterion. Although
there is no *good* significance test for finding out if
there is bias beyond this regression artifact, one may
find the procedures of Jöreskog (1978) or Hidiroglou et
al. (1979) useful as descriptive devices for disattenuating these slopes.

     Further complex analyses involve many control vari-
ables or predictors. The Bayer and Astin article (1975)
is one, and this has been discussed elsewhere (Wolins
1978). However, these more complex analyses may be conceptually reduced to the simple case. One may conceive of
a $\hat{Y}$ derived from an optimally weighted composite of fallible (of course) control variables. This $\hat{Y}$ (a variable) is
the fallible control variable and the regression artifact
results from it.

     Other mistakes of this kind occur in the general lit-
erature and they are advocated in technical articles
(Smith 1976) and textbooks (Kirk 1968). For example, Kirk
recommends that if groups differ on several dependent
variables, one should test if one of them is significant
when the other is controlled. Although such results may
be useful descriptively, that is, whether group differences grow smaller or larger or whether groups change
their order, the use of these results is a dangerous recommendation because:

1.   Groups may differ on both Ys for the same reason--
     both Ys may be significant when the other is con-
     trolled because each Y is fallible from a measurement
     point of view and the composite of the two may better
     discriminate between groups because of increased re-
     liability.

2.   Groups may differ on both Ys for different reasons
     but, because of the fallibility, it may appear that
     only one of these dependent variables is discriminat-
     ing between groups. This is illustrated in Fig. 2.1.
     When Y_1 is the fallible measure, the dotted line rep-
     resents the common slope. When Y_1' represents the in-
     fallible measure, the solid line represents the

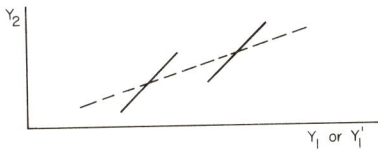

Fig. 2.1. Different slopes for errorful (Y_1-dotted) line vs. errorless (Y_1'-solid line) control variable resulting in apparent lack of group differences when such differences exist.

common slope. In the latter case group differences for Y_2 are present whereas they appear not to be present when the fallible Y_1 is used for control.

Again there is no good way to test such hypotheses, but correlations and plots may be informative as well as the disattenuation procedures previously cited.

A variation of this mistake is also pervasive. It involves the comparison of profiles. It occurs when certain parents are shown the profile of their children's achievement scores and in comparisons of Wechsler profiles of senile and nonsenile old people by Morrison (1976).

One reason the mistake may occur is because subtests in a battery are not equally reliable. Subtests in a battery have the same total variance but, when unequally reliable, have unequal true and error variance. For example, according to the Wechsler manual (1958), picture completion has a reliability of .83 and information has a reliability of .92. These reliabilities reflect proportion of true variance. Thus if a senile group differs from a nonsenile group in level of profile, one should expect nonparallel profiles: that is, if senility lowers general intelligence rather than some specific trait, one should expect the information subtest to be lowered more than the picture completion subtest because it is more reliable or more sensitive to differences in general intelligence. The analyses by Morrison (1976) invite one to infer that senility lowers the whole profile, rather than one subtest more than another. If one disattenuates the measures, the results indicate that information and arithmetic are reduced less by senility than are similarities and picture completion. Later discussion indicates there are further problems with this inference and that profile analysis based on fallible measures may be meaningless when the profiles differ in level.

Similar artifacts occur when inspecting profiles of achievement tests for school children. Achievement measures of arithmetic are typically highly reliable whereas measures of social studies are less so. Thus it will appear that children with relatively high profiles are better in arithmetic than social studies whereas children with low profiles will appear to perform better in social studies.

This artifact has also been instrumental in the diagnosis of sociopathy by means of the Wechsler profile. Many studies indicate that sociopaths score better on the performance part of this intelligence test, but the performance part is less reliable than the verbal part and sociopaths tend to have low profiles. This criticism has been offered in the literature. However, Brody and Brody (1976) have summarized the studies dealing with this topic and if one makes a scatterplot of the mean performance of the two measures across the many studies, one finds that this profile does not occur for studies where the sociopaths have IQs within the normal range.

Another example of this variety of RTMM comes from a study by Lewis and St. John (1974). There is a problem with the sample in this study that is discussed in Chapter 4. Basically these authors deal with black and white children in many desegregated classrooms, some of which contain mostly white children and others of which contain predominantly black children. The dependent variable is scholastic achievement and they hypothesize that peer ratings derived from the majority group will be more predictive of scholastic achievement than peer ratings derived from the minority group, and indeed they did find this true. They report: "black achievement is significantly related to popularity with blacks, not whites, in majority-black settings, and with whites, not blacks, in majority-white settings." This statement is based on significance tests applied to partial regression coefficients in which the achievement measure was regressed on the average of the ratings from two sources; black and white children. These authors did not take into account that these two popularity indices are not equally reliable. From the method section of that article it would appear that the popularity index for the blacks in majority-black settings would be based on about 14 black children whereas comparable ratings for these black children from whites would be based on about 5 children. Similarly, in majority white-settings each black child would have ratings from about 20 whites and 7 blacks. Since the number of raters does influence the reliability of the average ratings in precisely the same way that the number of items in a test influence the reliability of a test and reliability does influence validity, it is clear that these results can be readily explained by unequal reliability rather than by the social-psychological reasons offered by the authors.

SUMMARY

What is the illogic behind these RTMMs? It is the apparent (only apparent) illogic of statistical thinking. Consider the example of a child with an IQ of 140. If we know nothing else about that child, the child's IQ should be taken at face value. We can do no better than estimating that child's IQ as 140. However, suppose we have additional information, not about the child, but about the group to which he belongs. Suppose we know that the average IQ of the children in the school he attends is 100. Given this piece of information--*not about the child*--the IQ of 140 is no longer an unbiased one. The best estimate is less than 140. How much less depends on how fallibly the IQ was measured and the measure is always fallible to some extent.

Not only is this apparently illogical, it is apparently unfair (maybe not apparently?). For example, if we knew that the child was black, the best estimate of his IQ would be less than if we knew he were white. It is not the knowledge of the child's race that allows this prediction but prior knowledge of the average IQ of these racial groups. Similarly, if we wished to predict grades in school with these IQ tests, we would obtain better predictions if we predicted lower grades for blacks than for whites when the IQ is controlled. This result is *not* the result of bias on the part of teachers in giving grades, although that might also occur, but is a necessary outcome of fallible measurement.

One may be outraged by this apparent illogic unfairness but that is the way things are. The statistical thinking is not ivory tower theorizing but results in accurate descriptions of experiential facts. Blacks do get lower grades than whites even though they have the same IQ and high IQ blacks score lower than comparably high scoring whites when tested again.

This thinking is outrageous, however, only because of fallible measurement. If our measurement were better, this apparent illogic would be less pronounced. Since we will be living with fallible measurement in the foreseeable future, we should at least keep in mind this apparent illogic and understand when and how it occurs even though the why of it may seem obscure.

REFERENCES

Antigullah, M. 1964. The robustness of the covariance analysis of a one-way classification. *Biometrika*, pp. 365-72.

Bayer, A. E., and H. S. Astin. 1975. Sex differentials in the academic reward system. *Science*, pp. 796-802.

Brody, E. B., and N. Brody. 1976. *Intelligence: Nature, Determinants, and Consequences*. New York: Academic Press.

Bruvold, W. H. 1973. Belief and behavior as determinants of attitude. *Journal of Social Psychology*, pp. 285-89.

Button, C. B. 1974. Political education for minority groups. In *The Politics of Future Citizens*, eds. R. G. Niemi and Assoc. San Francisco: Jossey-Bass

Campbell, D. T., and A. Erlebacher. 1970. How regression artifacts in quasi-experimental evaluations can mistakenly make compensatory education look harmful. *Disadvantaged Child*, pp. 185-210.

Campbell, D. T., and D. W. Fiske. 1959. Convergent and discriminant validation by the multitrait-multimethod matrix. *Psychological Bulletin*, pp. 81-105.

Cohen, J., and P. Cohen. 1975. *Applied Multiple Regression/Correlation Analysis for the Behavioral Sciences*. Hillsdale, N. J.: Lawrence Erlbaum Assoc.

Edelson, I. E., and E. Seidman. 1975. Use of video taped feedback in altering interpersonal perceptions of married couples: a therapy analogue. *Journal of Consulting and Clinical Psychology*, pp. 244-50.

Hamilton, B. L. 1976. A Monte Carlo test of the robustness of parametric and non parametric analysis of covariance against unequal regression slopes. *Journal of the American Statistical Association*, pp. 864-69.

------. 1977. An empirical investigation of the effects of heterogeneous regression slopes in analysis of covariance. *Educational and Psychological Measurement*, pp. 701-12.

Hidiroglou, M. A., W. A. Fuller, and R. D. Hickman. 1979
     Super Carp. Ames: Survey Section, Statistical Lab-
     oratory, Iowa State University.

Jöreskog, K. G., and D. Sorbom. 1978. *LISREL IV-A Com-
     puter Program for Estimation of a Linear Structural
     Equation System by Maximum Likelihood Methods*.
     Chicago: National Educational Resources.

Kirk, R. E. 1968. *Experimental Design*. Monterey,
     Calif.: Brooks/Cole.

Lewis, R., and N. St. John. 1974. Contribution of cross-
     cultural friendship to minority group achievement in
     desegregated classrooms. *Sociometry*, pp. 79-91.

Lord, F. M. 1967. A paradox in the interpretation of
     group comparisons. *Psychological Bulletin*, pp. 304-
     5.

Morrison, D. F. 1976. *Multivariate Statistical Methods*.
     New York: McGraw-Hill.

Mosteller, F., and J. W. Tukey. 1977. *Data Analysis and
     Regression*. Reading, Mass.: Addison-Wesley.

Smith, J. C. 1976. Psychotherapeutic effects of trans-
     cendental meditation with controls for expectation of
     relief and daily sitting. *Journal of Consulting and
     Clinical Psychology*, pp. 630-37.

Wechsler, D. 1958. *Measurement and Appraisal of Adult
     Intelligence*, 4th ed. Baltimore: Williams and
     Wikins.

Wildt, A. R., and O. T. Ahtola. 1978. *Analysis of Co-
     variance*. Beverly Hills, Calif.: Sage Publ.

Willerman, Lee. 1979. *The Psychology of Individual and
     Group Differences*. San Francisco: W. H. Freeman.

Wolins, L. 1978. Sex differentials in salary. *Science*,
     pp. 723.

Woodward, J. A., and M. J. Goldstein. 1977. Communica-
     tion deviance in families of schizophrenics: A com-
     ment on the misuse of covariance. *Science*, pp. 1096-
     97.

3

Scale Dependent Mistakes

Two recent articles on the Scale Dependent Mistake (SDM) have been published by Wolins (1978, 1981) and Gaito (1980) and Busemeyer (1980) have each published lately on this topic. Of course, the SDM has a long history and the references in these articles should provide a starting point if one wishes to pursue the topic. However, the impact of SDMs on specific psychological research problems is discussed by Wolins (1978, 1981) only in regard to cognitive measures and not at all by others. Thus the researcher in applied areas is invited to conclude that this heated controversy about scales is purely academic and has no bearing on the everyday problems of the social scientist who applies them. This would be true if the arguments did not infiltrate the applied literature by way of statistics and measurement textbooks. Both Gaito (1980) and Wolins (1978) discuss this aspect, but the problem may be caricaturized as follows. S. S. Stevens (1951), a famous psychologist, tore loose a concept from its roots in physics and laid it on to psychology. Without roots it rotted and made a big stink. We are still trying to clean up the mess. I have looked at the mess in one area; I now look elsewhere. First, the concept must be defined. There is no theoretical basis in most areas of the social and behavioral sciences for comparing differences when those differences occur at different places on a scale. If one wishes to compare differences on different parts of a scale one must use an empirical basis. This very basic idea is thoroughly discussed by Cronbach (1970) and is central to many of the quasi-experimental designs offered by Campbell and Stanley (1966). However these authors do not really get into the scaling problem;

so the erroneous ideas offered by Stevens and perpetuated
in these textbooks have not been integrated with the admonitions offered by Cronbach, Campbell and Stanley, and
others.

Since the reader has been offered these citations and
the topic is dealt with in the recent literature, let it
suffice here to consider a textbook example (Morrison
1976) that is instructive in two ways and to discuss two
recent articles to show that the misconception still prevails. In addition some problems related to analysis of
covariance and nonrandom assignment will be addressed.

PROFILE ANALYSIS
        Morrison states, in addition to the other assumptions
of Multivariate Analysis of Variance (MANOVA), that commensurability is required to make a profile analysis.
Commensurability means that the units of measurement in
the various dependent variable are the same. By this definition it would be appropriate to compare two population
profiles in which the dependent variables are shoe size,
hat size, height, and girth-at-the-waist, since all of
these variables can be measured in inches and these other
assumptions of MANOVA place no restrictions on the vari-
ance-covariance structure. However, in this context it is
easily noted that variance in height will be much greater
than variance in hat or shoe size. Thus parallel profiles
would be a very unusual condition indeed. That is, if two
populations differed in size, one would be very surprised
if the difference between them in inches was the same for
hat size as for height. Further, girth in particular is
suspect as a measure of size since it may also reflect
obesity. Thus girth, though commensurable with the other
measures (and probably positively correlated with them),
may result in differences in the profiles because of differences in obesity rather than differences in the general
concept of structural size.
        This ludicrous example should make it clear that com-
mensurability, though necessary, does not suffice for the
reasonable application of profile analysis. Thus the
question arises, if commensurability does not suffice,
what are the sufficient conditions?
        Commensurability in the social sciences might imply
that the variances in some normative population are equal.
Without equality of variances we might have the incongru-
ous comparison of hat size differences with height

differences. In Wechsler's Adult Intelligence Scale
(WAIS) it may seem all right if the subtests scores are
reported in standard scores because all subtests were
standardized on the same population. A problem with this
is that equal variances for subtests in a normative population need not imply equal variances for the special
groups being investigated (Wechsler 1958). That is, the
old people used in the Morrison example may be more or
less variable with respect to any one of the subtests.

The commensurability condition might hold, for example, if the two groups consisted of random samples from
the standardization population who were treated differently. However, the only sampling information we have from
Morrison's presentation is that the participants were
"Forty-nine elderly men participating in an interdisci-
plinary study of human aging. . . ." Thus it is not clear
that commensurability exists in the data used by Morrison.
In addition, it appears that the observed variances on the
four subtests, adjusted for group differences, are unequal. If the obtained variances were unequal but commensurability and equal variance were known to exist in some
normative sense, the unequal variability observed would
not be of particular concern in the analysis of profiles.
However, in context of the problem Morrison defines, commensurability is not necessarily present so that the ap-
pearance of unequal variance detracts from the credibility
of commensurability.

The dependent variables must be nonzero correlated
for MANOVA to be reasonable because MANOVA may have no advantage over simple univariate analyses if the dependent
variables are zero correlated. When the dependent variables are zero correlated, MANOVA may give a more powerful
overall test as well as protection against type II error,
but the multivariate confidence intervals will be at least
as large as the univariate ones. Similarly if the variances are equal and the covariances are equal, the univariate analysis of variance for repeated measures is better than MANOVA. Thus the primary advantage of MANOVA
occurs when the dependent variables are nonzero correlated
but not homogeneously.

Although MANOVA makes no assumptions about the covariance structure, meaningful interpretation of profile
analysis requires some consideration of this. First consider what we know about WAIS subtests (Wechsler 1958;
Reschly 1978):

1. The subtests correlate positively but not homoge-
    neously. Although all tests tend to load on a gener-
    al factor, albeit unequally, three of the four sub-
    tests load on a verbal factor and the fourth, like
    girth in the ludicruous example, loads on a perform-
    ance factor.

2. For each subtest the reliabilities substantially ex-
    ceed the correlations among the subtests, indicating
    each subtest measures something unique even though
    each shares some common variance.

3. The covariance structure varies from population to
    population depending on such variables as age, educa-
    tion, and social status.

Given these three facts, but, for simplicity, assum-
ing equal variances and equal measurement error, we might
conclude from a significant outcome that the differences
between the groups are different with respect to: (1)
general intelligence only, but since this factor is measured better by some subtests than others, profile differences should appear even when senility results in lowering
only general intelligence; (2) verbal and performance, the
two factors that occur when the WAIS is factor analyzed;
(3) the unique variance in each measure; and (4) any of
the above.

It is obvious that similar explanations could be
given for a nonsignificant outcome. That is, there could
be compensating effects so that the profiles would appear
parallel even when substantial differences in the traits
measured by the variables exist.

To illustrate the ambiguity of the results of profile
analysis and to show that these covariance considerations
are not avoiding the issue of whether the WAIS subtests
are diagnostic of senility in old people, consider another
possible result involving four dependent variables and two
groups where the profiles are precisely parallel so that
the F statistic is precisely zero. Also suppose that the
covariance matrix is

$$\begin{bmatrix} 10 & 5 & -5 & -5 \\ & 10 & -5 & -5 \\ & & 10 & 5 \\ & & & 10 \end{bmatrix}$$

This covariance matrix is assumed to be the same for each group and for each group the sample covariance matrix is supposed to estimate the population covariance matrix. However, this covariance matrix indicates that in the general population people low on variables 1 and 2 will tend to be high on variables 3 and 4 and vice versa. As a result, if the overall F statistic is significant, a nondiagnostic result would occur if the group highest on variables 1 and 2 was lowest on variables 3 and 4 as indicated by the negative correlations between these two sets of variables. But given these negative correlations and parallel profiles, one should infer that the variables are diagnostic because the covariance structure indicates if the profiles are not the same, they cross for the general population but do not cross for the two samples because they are parallel.

It is surely true that the hypothesis of parallel profiles will be rejected more often than not by social scientists because of scale artifacts rather than substantive reasons. Thus unequal variances, unequal measurement error, or the particular covariance structure could be instrumental in producing significant results. Consequently the investigator acquires no information from doing profile analysis.

It is unfortunate for this criticism that the results of the analysis Morrison uses to illustrate profile analysis leads to the correct inference, for it appears that the shape of the WAIS profile is not useful for diagnosing senility or anything else (Brody and Brody 1976, pp. 219-25). This argument against profile analysis would appear more convincing if significant results had occurred because these scale problems should more likely produce significant results. However, it is clear from Morrison's presentation that the hypothesis being tested was whether the shape of the WAIS profile is diagnostic of senility. Therefore he would infer that the WAIS profile is diagnostic of senility if the test were significant; that inference could not be reasonable, given these scale problems.

Commensurability, like interval measurement (Wolins 1978) is meaningless in the context of social-behavioral science variables. If our scales do not have equal units, it is not reasonable to expect the units to be comparable from one scale to another. Using the same normative group insures us only of comparable units in some average sense. But if two variables share only part of their variance, we have no assurance of comparable units at any particular

place in scales. For example, in one scale the units may
be small in one place and large in another place. This
inequality of units may be related to the size of the measurement error at that particular location on the scale as
dictated by the item difficulties or it may be due to the
particular combination of traits being measured at that
location as dictated by the content of the items discrimi-
nating there.

A further consideration is that the procedure offered
by Morrison does have application in some contexts. For
example, if the observational units were automobiles, the
groups were defined as deisel engines versus gasoline engines, and the dependent variables were cost per mile for
different driving conditions, the method Morrison employs
would be right for answering the relevant questions. Of
the previous concerns only unequal measurement error has
any potential for clouding the results. Equality of variances or the covariance structure would not be relevant if
one were choosing a type of engine for a particular set of
driving conditions. Thus the method Morrison employed is
not wrong but the application is. Morrison, a statistician, neither understood the question of the diagnostic
value of the WAIS nor appreciated the attributes of the
measures used in the social-behavioral sciences. This
problem seems to permeate the application of statistics in
the social-behavioral sciences.

The second aspect of this mistaken use of commensurability that is instructive in that it illustrates a
breakdown in communication between the consultant and the
client. Morrison acknowledges several individuals who
were responsible for formulating the problem and collecting the data. I presume these individuals were social
scientists and therefore one might expect that these social scientists could have done a better job of communi-
cating to Morrison the properties of WAIS subtests. However, such expectations are unrealistic. Their unreality
reinforces my opinion that social scientists are under-
trained in the areas of measurement and statistics.

One or the other or preferably both of those involved in a client-consultant relationship needs to be familiar with the psychological and statistical aspects of the
problem. Since the research was psychological, and it is
not reasonable to expect statisticians to be educated in
other disciplines, it is my judgment that Morrison was
lead astray by the psychologists rather than the other
way. On the other hand, Morrison might have presented

more clearly the implications of commensurability.

TWO EXAMPLES
     I have been able to find in the current literature
only one use of profile analysis in MANOVA (Gray-Toft
1980), but two articles appeared in the last year (Gentry
and Zimring 1979; Staw and Ross 1980) that illustrate this
same misconception in the univariate context. Both articles interpret, without qualification, the presence of a
significant interaction in the presence of main effects.
Gentry and Zimring find that speech is less intelligible
when background noise is present and that staff members at
an institution understand speech better than the developmentally disabled residents. They also conclude that
"specific acoustic environments . . . are even more important for residents." Under the two noise conditions
the percent correct for staff are about 70 percent and 90
percent; for the residents they are about 30 percent and
60 percent. In the Staw and Ross study the rated performance of subjects was higher when they experienced success
rather than failure and when they were instructed to take
a consistent course of action rather than an experimenting
one. The normalized scores for the consistent condition
for failure and success were -.92 and 2.06; for the experimenting condition they were -1.38 and .34.
     In neither case would I object to the analysis if the
results were properly qualified. For example, Torgesen
and Houch (1980) report conceptually similar results but
they offer their audience an excellent discussion of why
the interaction could result from the scale and tell them
that the data does not necessarily support the apparent
inference.

A SPECIAL CASE
     In the late seventies two very similar articles ap-
peared (Rubin 1977; Overall and Woodward 1977) indicating
that the analysis of covariance is not a biased procedure,
as discussed in Chapter 2, when the OUs are nonrandomly
assigned to treatments on the basis of the covariate. An
extreme example of this would be to give a group of children an IQ test, to split the group at the median, and to
assign the lower group to a Head Start treatment and use
the upper group as control. The analysis that is suppos-
edly unbiased is the usual regression analysis for the

partial regression coefficient for the dummy variable designating treatment groups in which IQ is controlled. The dependent variable might be an achievement test following treatment or grades in school. However, the analysis of covariance is effective in this context only when the control variable correlates substantially with the dependent one, as it surely does in this context. Since it does, the variability in one group takes place over a different portion of both scales than the variability of the other group. Since this is the case, one is looking at the interaction of IQ with achievement in which both main effects are significant. This is conceptually identical to the mistakes previously discussed. The groups differ in IQ because we selected them that way. Since they differ in IQ, they almost certainly will differ in achievement since such results are predictable on the basis of a large amount of experience. Thus the question addressed: Is the difference in achievement predictable from the difference in IQ? As these authors indicate, regression toward the mean does not produce bias as discussed in Chapter 2, but the analysis is indefensible on the basis of this chapter. The subjects in the two groups vary over different portions of the scale, and the intervals are not necessarily equal.

Actually Rubin does a reasonable job of pointing this out but Overall and Woodward fail to mention the problem. Yet the problem is insurmountable, given our present theory and technology. So I ask: What is the merit of giving journal space in applied social science journals to topics with no practical application? My answer is that it has negative merit since these publications encourage misuse.

SUMMARY

As was the case in Chapter 2, these SDMs are prevalent because they are inconsistent with our everyday experiences. Numbers usually reflect magnitude, but in our everyday experiences we do not question where the numbers come from. Usually it is fairly obvious and other times it is too technical for us to afford the time to understand. As scientists we must understand where our numbers come from. As social scientists we must understand the limitations imposed by our lack of strong theory and depend instead on experience in interpreting numbers.

When experience is lacking, sometimes statistics helps. For example, composites derived from many numbers with ordinal properties tend to be nicely distributed so that we may legitmately do parametric analysis. Yet statistics will not help us to attach meaning to these averages. This meaning must come from *our* research and *our* theory. We cannot and should not hope for any help from the statistician in this regard.

Finally, the units in which a measure is reported are not important. In the case of the diesel and gasoline automobiles I could, if necessary, change miles to kilometers. What is important is that the measures have the same meaning and distance-covered-per-unit-of-cost-of-fuel does have the same meaning for different cars and driving conditions. However, I do not believe one could convincingly argue this for the WAIS and the old people.

REFERENCES

Brody, E. B., and N. Brody. 1976. *Intelligence: Nature, Determinants, and Consequences*. New York: Academic Press.

Busemeyer, J. R. 1980. Importance of measurement theory, error theory, and experimental design for testing the significance of interactions. *Psychological Bulletin*, pp. 237-44.

Campbell, D. T., and J. C. Stanley. 1966. *Experimental and Quasi-experimental Designs for Research*. Chicago: Rand McNally.

Cronbach, L. J., and L. Furby. 1970. How we should measure "change" . . . or should we? *Psychological Bulletin*, pp. 68-80.

Gaito, John. 1980. Measurement scales and statistics: Resurgence of an old misconception. *Psychological Bulletin*, pp. 564-67.

Gentry, D. M., and C. M. Zimring. 1979. Effects of institutional room acoustics on speech discrimination of developmentally disabled residents and of staff. *Journal of Applied Psychology*, pp. 541-47.

Gray-Toft, P. 1980. Effectiveness of a counseling support program for hospice nurses. *Journal of Counseling Psychology*, pp. 346-54.

Morrison, D. F. 1976. *Multivariate Statistical Methods*. New York: McGraw-Hill.

Overall, J. E., and J. A. Woodward. 1977. Nonrandom assignment and the analysis of covariance. *Psychological Bulletin*, pp. 588-94.

Reschly, D. J. 1978. WISC–R factor structures among anglos, blacks, chicanos and native-american papagos.
Journal of Consulting Psychology, pp. 417-22.

Rubin, D. B. 1977. Assignment to treatment groups on the
basis of a covariate. *Journal of Educational Statistics*, pp. 1-26.

Staw, B. M., and J. Ross. 1980. Commitment in an experimenting society: A study of the attribution of lead-
ership from administrative scenarios. *Journal of
Applied Psychology*, pp. 249-60.

Stevens, S. S. 1951. Mathematics, measurement, and psy-
chophysics. ed. S. S. Stevens. *Handbook of Experimental Psychology*. New York: Wiley.

Torgesen, J. K., and D. G. Houck. 1980. Processing defi-
ciencies of learning-disabled children who perform
poorly on the digit span test. *Journal of Educational Psychology*, pp. 141-60.

Wechsler, D. 1958. *The Measurement and Appraisal of
Adult Intelligence*. 4th ed. Baltimore: Williams
and Wilkins.

Wolins, L. 1978. Interval measurement: Physics, psycho-
physics and metaphysics. *Educational and Psychological Measurement*, pp. 1-9.

------. 1981. Reanalyzing studies of race differences in
intelligence. In *Reanalyzing Program Evaluations*.
eds. R. F. Boruch, P. M. Wortman, and D. F. Cordray
and Assoc. San Francisco: Jossey-Bass.

4

Variable and Observational Unit Mistakes

Research involves collecting OUs, measuring these OUs on a variable or variables for some designated purpose or purposes, and analysis. The Variable and Observational Unit Mistake (VOUM) involves a breakdown in logic between the OU and the purpose or the analysis.

There appear to be three varieties of VOUMs plus a miscellaneous assortment. In this chapter an attempt will be made to delineate each variety using some well known statistical models and to give some examples of each variety as well as examples of miscellaneous VOUMs. Finally, a defense of the logical coherence of these kinds of mistakes will be undertaken.

The first variety ($VOUM_1$) occurs when either the OUs include more than one individual (e.g., married couples, identical twins), or the OUs are repeatedly measured (e.g., trials in a learning experiment, several observers or judges responding to the same individual's behaviors), and the OUs are randomly assigned to treatment groups. Under these circumstances the test for treatment differences requires a different error term than the test for the repeated measures and interaction. The mistake is testing all three effects with a combined error term.

The second variety ($VOUM_2$) involves the same data setup but two error terms are used. However, the data do not conform to the analysis of variance model and other analyses are better in several different ways.

The third variety ($VOUM_3$) involves individuals nested within some groups (e.g., students within classrooms, workers within plants); the purpose of the research is to evaluate groups (classrooms or plants) but the analysis is

based on only individuals. We shall be concerned with
multivariate situations in which each individual responds
to one set of stimuli, but unlike the previously described
VOUMs, these stimuli are not the same: they are usually
attitude or questionnaire items. We shall not deal with
the simple $VOUM_3$ because we appear to have almost outgrown
it. One no longer finds in the literature experiments in
which one teacher teaches a classroom under a certain condition and another teacher teaches another classroom under
a second condition and then a t-test is performed on the
basis of individual scores to determine if the conditions
vary. However, Button's (1974) study is almost as dis-
torted.

$VOUM_1$

        The Edelson and Seidman (1975) study is an example of
a $VOUM_1$. The OU was a married couple. A reasonable analysis would have involved two error terms--one for treatments and another for sex and sex by treatment--but only
the one combined error term was used. A more important
$VOUM_1$ was offered to me by my colleague Mildred Mason.

Stanley and Hall (1973) observes 66 subjects in two treatment groups (G) in which each subject (S) performs three
tasks (T). They report significant group effects but not
significant task and interaction effects. For each test
the error degrees of freedom (df) were 192. This is ex-
actly what one should expect under null conditions given
only the almost universal finding of some reliability of
measurement or measureable individual differences. This
study is more important than that by Edelson and Seidman
because Naylor (1980) cites Stanley and Hall in a review
article.

Table 4.1. An analysis for the Stanley and Hall data

Source	df	Expected Mean Square
G	1	$\sigma_e^2 + 3\sigma_S^2 + 99K_G^2$
S/G	64	$\sigma_e^2 + 3\sigma_S^2$
T	2	$\sigma_e^2 + 66K_T^2$
GT	2	$\sigma_e^2 + 33K_{GT}^2$
e	128	σ_e^2

Table 4.2. An analysis for the Stanley and Hall data under null conditions

Source	df	Expected Mean Square
G	1	$\sigma_e^2 + 3\sigma_S^2$
S/G	64	$\sigma_e^2 + 3\sigma_S^2$
T	2	σ_e^2
GT	2	σ_e^2
e	128	σ_e^2

Let us explore why the results reported by Stanley and Hall are expected under null conditions. A reasonable model for the data might be

$$Y_{ijk} = G_i + S_{ij} + T_k + (GT)_{ik} + e_{ijk}$$

where $S_{ij} \sim NID(0,\sigma_S^2)$. Given the model, the analysis should be as in Table 4.1.

Let us suppose, for the purpose of the experiment, that null conditions imply $K_G^2 = K_T^2 = K_{GT}^2 = 0$ so that we have the results in Table 4.2. Given Table 4.2 results and what Stanley and Hall actually did, one can derive the results given in Table 4.3.

It is evident that the F ratios for groups is expected to be greater than 1, and the other two Fs are expected to be less than 1.

VOUM$_2$

If the model for the Stanley and Hall study is correct, the covariances among the three tasks over the 33 subjects in each group should have the structure given in Table 4.4.

Table 4.3. The Stanley and Hall analysis under null conditions

Source	df	Expected Mean Square
G	1	$\sigma_e^2 + 3\sigma_S^2$
T	2	σ_e^2
GT	2	σ_e^2
"error"	192	$\sigma_e^2 + \sigma_S^2$

Table 4.4. Expected covariances among tasks for each group

	T_1	T_2	T_3
T_1	$\sigma_e^2 + \sigma_s^2$	σ_s^2	σ_s^2
T_2	σ_s^2	$\sigma_e^2 + \sigma_s^2$	σ_s^2
T_3	σ_s^2	σ_s^2	$\sigma_e^2 + \sigma_s^2$

One may actually compute the mean squares by obtaining the pooled-within-group covariance matrix and operating on it (Dickinson and Wolins 1974), but one should not pool these matrices unless one expects them to be the same under null conditions. The test statistic does not require that these matrices be the same under nonnull conditions. But if they are not the same, only the test is legitimate--estimates of the variance components and statistics derived from the noncentral F distribution are no longer correct. In addition, if the covariances change as a function of the means, then ignoring this change is a PSAP--the covariances potentially contain information about location. This is discussed by Hanser et al. (1979).

Over the years I have inspected hundreds of such matrices derived from educational and learning experiments in which subjects are observed over time and I have never seen one that appears to meet the structural requirements portrayed in Table 4.4. What I *always* see is that measures taken close in time correlate higher than measures taken widely apart in time--adjacent measures correlate highly and the correlations go down as the number of time periods that intervene between two measures increase. This trend is less obvious when performance stabilizes or asymptotes. That is, if the means toward the end of the series of trials are similar, the correlations toward the end of the series tend to be uniformally high.

It is also generally observed that the variances change with the mean in a systematic way. Most often the variance is largest on the first trial and grows systematically smaller over trials. Sometimes the variances are largest in the middle of a series, particularly when the composite learning curve appears to be ogive.

When the prescribed structure (Table 4.4) is not realized and the covariance matrices are not the same under nonnull conditions, a different mode of analysis is suggested. In learning experiments the analysis given in Table 4.1 is inefficient for two reasons. First, the trials are ordered in time and the analysis does not use this information. Second, under nonnull conditions the experimenter should expect both group differences and group-by-trial interaction. That is, the better learning condition should become increasingly effective over trials because a better learning condition should increase the rate of learning. Thus a single outcome from a learning perspective requires two significance tests and the power of the experiment is thereby reduced.

If only a few time periods are involved, the MANOVA is a better way for handling the data. Even if one had only three trials, one might fit a quadratic function for each subject and derive for each subject an intercept, a linear, and a quadratic coefficient. Then one can do the MANOVA using these coefficients. Either way the MANOVA test will come out the same. Most often only the linear and intercept are significant, and the polynomial fitting is thereby more informative.

With many trials one might still do the MANOVA using only the quadratic fit and thereby more efficiently reduce the df than by means of the Greenhouse-Geisser correction (1959).

Each one of the univariate tests on the coefficients are robust against the usual assumptions but unfortunately they are correlated. People who learn quickly tend to have high intercepts and high linear and low quadratic coefficients as compared to slow learners. Consequently the univariate tests are less powerful than the multivariate one. These correlations will not generally be the same from group to group under nonnull conditions so that the MANOVA is not sufficient. Yet the coefficients of the polynomials, which are averaged for each treatment group, can be scrutinized by the researcher. Such coefficients may provide a succinct description of the group differences.

Finally, in the context of unequal covariance matrices I refer the reader to Chapter 1; with small samples and no control on sample sizes, unequal covariance matrices can invalidate even the significance test. It is the Behrens-Fisher problem but larger.

VOUM$_3$

VOUM$_3$s are also extremely prevalent. The study by Stern (1970) and its criticism (Layton 1972) have been cited; so the discussion will begin with the study by Kennedy (1975), since much research is being conducted on evaluation of faculty performance and much of it is wrong in the way Layton (1972) describes. Following this, the focus will be on a study by Brown (1976), who for subtle reasons presents ambiguous results.

When one asks if the way a student evaluates an instructor is related to the way the instructor grades the student, one may ask this question in two contexts: within classrooms and between classrooms. They are conceptually independent questions. For example, it is possible that within the average classroom these two variables correlate -1 whereas the means for each classroom might correlate +1. This situation is depicted in Fig. 4.1. The subtle aspect of the situation is that these relationships are not actually independent even though the result depicted in Fig. 4.1 is possible. Specifically, for any multivariately measured population, the expectation under null conditions of the between-covariance matrix is the same as the within-covariance matrix (Morrison 1976). That is, if the grades instructors give depend only on the student (not on the instructor, etc.) and the evaluations that students give depend only on the student and students are randomly assigned to instructors, one expects the correlation for any one classroom to be the same as the correlation of the means across classrooms.

What Kennedy did was to analyze results for several hundred students in 30 sections of a course taught by 15 instructors. He used the student as the unit of analysis without regard to either section or instructor and reported that students with higher grades evaluated their instructors higher. We do not know from these results if the significant result achieved is due to individual differences, or instructor differences, or a combination of these.

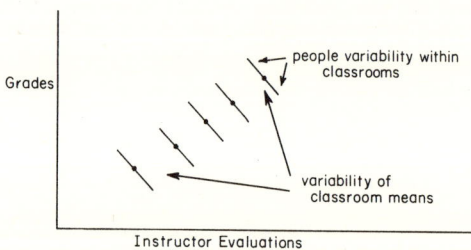

Fig. 4.1. Possible different relationship between two variables depending on the observational unit.

Brown (1976) did not make this mistake. Even though he analyzed sections rather than instructors, the results convincingly demonstrate that grades and evaluations are positively related between classrooms. The question remains: Is this correlation due to individual variation that might randomly occur between classrooms or can it be attributed to the instructor or section? If the within-section two by two covariance matrix is of the same magnitude as the between-section two by two covariance matrix, one cannot infer that instructors who grade liberally are evaluated higher by their students. It is possible that on the average all instructors are evaluated the same, but individual differences within classrooms produce the between-classroom variability only because there are different individuals in each classroom and the correlations between the classroom means on these two variables merely reflect these individual differences.

Most of the contingency chi-square misuses cited by Lewis and Burke (1949) are $VOUM_3$s. Braunstein et al. (1973) present a more recent misuse as misleading as any of those cited by Lewis and Burke. They involve both a $VOUM_3$ and a miscellaneous VOUM. First, they analyze 27 classrooms even though the treatment was applied to 19 professors. Classrooms are nested within professors. Later they do a chi-square based on 117 responses from students in these 27 classes but it appears that the OU from which the count of 117 came is the questionnaire items. That is, for each classroom (27 of them) they looked at each of the 23 items to see if there was a change in the mean from the middle to the end of the semester of at least one scale point on the five-point Likert scale. Apparently 117 of the possible 621 changed this much. These 117 were presented in a 2×2 contingency table broken down by experimental vs. control and positive change vs. negative change. The chi-square was significant, which is not necessarily a rare event when the counts are highly correlated.

MISCELLANEOUS VOUM

A dramatic VOUM was reported by Al Rossiter, Jr., United Press International Science editor, in the *Ames Daily Tribune*, January 16, 1979. "A new study shows a mother's smoking significantly increases the risk of miscarriage and crib death, but does not, as generally

believed, affect a child's intelligence or long-term growth." He also commented, "the societal impact of these major birth defects was not great because most of the affected infants died before birth or right after birth."

The general implication of this report is that anom-
alies in children of mothers who smoked during pregnancy
should not be attributed to their mothers' smoking since
on the average those who survive this prenatal environment
are similar to the children whose mothers did not smoke.
But these results do not indicate that conclusion. I am
concerned that those who did not survive the adverse prenatal environment were genetically less viable, and there
is much data to indicate viability is related to IQ and
physical growth. Therefore it follows that if the less
viable are eliminated and IQ and growth are not affected
by mothers smoking, the survivors should exceed the average IQ and growth of the unselected children of nonsmoking
mothers. The only way the inference could be justified is
if the genetic variability with respect to IQ and growth
of those who died was identical to that of the survivors.

Another loose class of VOUMs that commonly occur is
that in which indices are derived from several samples and
these indices are correlated. For example, an intelligence test with n items might be administered to samples
from three populations where $N_1 = 100$, $N_2 = 200$ and $N_3 =
300$. The difficulty of each item is obtained from each
sample and the three samples are correlated across indices
to determine if two of the samples are more alike in their
pattern of item responses than either one is like the
third sample. Under null conditions, $r_{23} > r_{13} > r_{12}$ simply because indices that are based on larger samples are
more reliable. One must correct for unequal sample size
(disattenuate) in order to make these correlations comparable. The way to do this is well known.

Consider the problem of comparing indices derived
from different populations in which a significance test is
made for each item. This might occur when a morale survey
is given to two work groups: salaried and hourly. In
this case one would expect the salaried group to be higher
on every item and a likely outcome would be that each item
is significant, reflecting the overall group differences.
A better way to summarize such data is to make a scatterplot of the item means, plotting the two groups against
each other. From this plot one may observe whether the
following conditions occur.

1.   The points are generally above or below a 45° line
     through the origin, which would indicate group dif-
     ferences in general morale.

2.   The points cluster along a line indicating the groups
     tend to have similar profiles of item responses.

3.   Certain points deviate from the main swarm of points
     indicating areas of morale for which the groups dif-
     fer independently of general morale.

4.   The item means are more variable for one group than
     another, indicating that the attitude being measured
     is more salient for one group than another. Of
     course this might be a scale artifact if the points
     are generally above or below the 45° line through the
     origin.

     Braunstein et al. (1973) could have used this proce-
dure rather than the uninformative chi-square based on 117
nonindependent observations. Six scatterplots for the 23
items could be constructed from the four measures of the
19 professors.
     Because of its pervasiveness, I do not feel compelled
to cite additional references for the latter VOUM, but Elrod and Crase (1980) illustrate the correct way to handle
such data when the number of groups are small.
     When the number of groups are small but the numbers
in each group are sizeable, inspection of the between- and
the within-group variability is essential. The inspection
of the scatterplot is complemented by the analysis of the
within-group variability. For example, if the pooled-
within group correlation matrix were factor analyzed and
one particular cluster of attitude items were thereby
identified, and if two groups differed on these items, as
determined from the scatterplot of the item means, one
should infer that the groups have different kinds of people in them rather than that the responses of the people
were caused by the group. On the other hand, if the cluster of items that distinguish among groups of people do
not occur in similar clusters from the factor analysis, it
may be reasonable to infer it is the grouping of the people that causes these response differences rather than the
groups having different kinds of people in them. More
specifically we may suppose we have surveyed two groups,
school board members and teachers, in several hundred

homogeneous communities. Next we do an analysis of variance for each item in an inventory and find that for the majority of the items neither the community nor the interaction of community with group is large but for many of the items there are large group differences. For all items we do the factor analysis for each group and find several factors that are similar for the two groups. Suppose a comparison of the means for the two groups reveals that the items loading on the traditional educational procedures factor have higher means for the school board members than for the teachers. From this we should infer that the groups differ on the same dimension as do individuals; perhaps the kind of people who run or get elected to school boards are more traditional than teachers. If some but not all of the items on the within-group factor distinguish between groups, or the items distinguishing between groups do not load highly on any within factor, then the basis for the difference is less likely to be due to the kind of people in groups and is more likely to be due to the particular interests or problems the groups confront.

If the number of groups are large, it would be profitable to perform factor analyses on both the between- and within-group covariance matrices. To the extent the pattern of between-group factor loadings are the same as the within-group factor loadings and the size of the loadings are similar, the groups do not differ on the common factors. If the inventory is so long that there is redundancy in the item content, no further analysis is required. For shorter inventories, it still may be informative to peruse the item means. If the pattern of loadings is the same for the between and within analyses but the between loadings are larger, one may infer the groups differ because they have different kinds of people in them. To the extent that between-group factors occur that have no counterpart from the within-group analysis, the groups differ on dimensions on which individuals do not differ and these differences are most likely to be intrinsic to the group.

It is also true that within-group factors may occur that have no counterpart from the between-group analysis. This can occur in an investigation or even when the OUs are randomly assigned to groups if these OUs are allowed to interact or are not treated independently. These within-group factors in the latter case can occur if various measures of popularity are obtained from peers, the teacher, and self ratings. Since it seems to be generally true for classrooms containing 20 or more individuals that cliques form and some members of the class are isolates, a general popularity factor can occur within groups but be less strong or nonexistent between groups. In an investigation the groups might be work groups in which each group is similarly structured according to job function so that there is heterogeneity in prestige and pay within--but not between--groups. As a result one might find that factor analyses of a morale survey produce a strong pay factor within--but not between--groups.

Lewis and St. John (1974) are guilty of a VOUM as well as the RTMM previously discussed. The independent variables were peer ratings and the errors are negatively correlated from a statistical point of view. When a rater is asked to select some specified number of peers from some small number of peers, we have a statistical problem similar to the problem of estimating the variance from a sample from a finite population. For the latter, the finite population correction is applied but there does not appear to be any simple solution for peer ratings. For one thing, each rater selects from his acquaintances so that the population size may vary from rater to rater. But these statistical problems are minor compared to the psychological ones. Ratees have a reputation that is communicated through a group by interactions among individuals. In the classroom situation, the interaction of the students with the teacher is observed by the whole class and is a potential source of nonindependence. The environment imposed by the teacher or teacher attributes, such as race in context of the Lewis and St. John study, are potential sources of nonindependence.

However, data derived from the 22 classrooms that vary in racial composition seem to be independent. A reasonable test of Lewis and St. John's hypothesis could be obtained by disattenuating the correlations of the peer ratings with grades (by recognizing the number of ratees of each race) for each classroom and then relating the difference or direction of the difference between the two disattenuated correlations to the racial composition of the classroom.

In this case the within-classroom variability is not informative because of the lack of statistical independence but this is not crucial in this context because racial composition of the classroom is a group variable and does not exist for the individual. Consequently the within-group analysis is at most ancillary to the purpose of the study.

SUMMARY
    It is clear that the reason we ask students to evalu-
ate instructors is to obtain a basis for evaluating the
instructor. It is clear that the reason we ask students
to respond to their academic environments is to obtain a
basis for evaluating that environment. It is clear that
part of the reason we subject students to different educational experiences is to evaluate these educational experiences.
    It is equally clear that students do not agree on
which instructors are good or bad, on how they perceive
their academic environment, and all students do not benefit equally from the same educational experiences even
when the overall benefits are the same.
    The integrity of the concept of VOUM when attempting
to evaluate group differences depends on confusing these
two sources of variability or ignoring individual differences. When individuals are repeatedly measured, individuals are not merely OUs, they are also variables, usually
random variables. They are part of the model. Variability caused by these differences among individuals provides
the key for answering questions about group differences.
    When individuals are repeatedly measured, individuals
are a recognized source of variability and not error. Error is a conglomerate of sources of variability that we do
not or cannot control. However, the error term for a particular effect is *not* necessarily the same thing as error.
It is never correct to decide on the error term after analyzing the data. The correct error term for a particular
effect, if there is one, depends on how the data were collected.
    When we repeatedly measure individuals, individual
differences are controlled when the comparison is between
the measures. Yet it often occurs that some of the effects in a single analysis occur between individuals and
individual differences must be included in the error term
for those effects. If one fails to do this, one will be
assured of significant results in the long run, given reliable measurement.
    In the univariate examples (VOUM$_1$) the mistake is
almost always getting the wrong error term by ignoring the

necessity of two error terms. In the multivariate examples (VOUM$_3$) the same conceptual mistake is made. The
authors fail to recognize that the responses of each student in one instructor's class is potentially a measure of
that instructor and a measure of that student. To some
extent students differ in the harshness or leniency of
their ratings, but one hopes they are also influenced by
the qualities of the instructor.

The study of smoking and nonsmoking mothers fit into
this class because the group differences that may occur
could be due to the kind of people who occur there, just
as is the case for instructor evaluations. Of course in
the former case we may label the mistake as selective at-
trition. However, whatever you call it, one is erroneous-
ly attributing the group differences (or in this case,
lack of group differences) to a specified variable when
other variables may be the more likely cause of the differences.

REFERENCES
Braunstein, D. N., G. A. Klein, and M. Pachla. 1973.
    Feedback expectancy in student ratings of college
    faculty. *Journal of Applied Psychology*, pp. 254-58.
Brown, D. L. 1976. Faculty ratings and student grades:
    A university-wide multiple regression analysis.
    Journal of Educational Psychology, pp. 573-78.
Button, C. D. 1974. Political education in minority
    groups. In *The Politics of Future Citizens*, eds.
    R. G. Niemi and Assoc. San Francisco: Jossey-Bass.
Dickinson, T. L., and L. Wolins. 1974. Least squares
    analysis of repeated measures and other designs.
    Multivariate Behavioral Research 9:353-71.
Edelson, I. E., and E. Seidman. 1975. Use of video taped
    feedback in altering interpersonal perceptions of
    married couples, a theory analogue. *Journal of Con-
    sulting and Clinical Psychology*, pp. 244-50.
Elrod, M. M., and S. J. Crase. 1980. Sex differences in
    self-esteem and parental behavior. *Psychological
    Reports*, pp. 719-27.
Greenhouse, S. W., and S. Geisser. 1959. On methods in
    the analysis of profile data. *Psychometrika*, pp. 95-
    112.
Hanser, L. M., R. M. Mendel, and L. Wolins. 1979. Three
    flies in the ointment: A reply to Arvey and Moss-
    holder. *Personnel Psychology*, pp. 511-16.

Kennedy, W. R. 1975. Grades expected and grades re-
    ceived--their relationship to students' evaluation of
    faculty performance. *Journal of Educational Psychol-
    ogy*, pp. 109-15.
Layton, W. L. 1972. Review of stern environmental index-
    es. In *The Seventh Mental Measurement Yearbook*, ed.
    O. K. Buros. Highland Park, N.J.: Gryphon Press.
Lewis, D., and C. J. Burke. 1949. The use and misuse of
    the chi-square test. *Psychological Bulletin*, pp.
    433-89.
Lewis, R., and N. St. John. 1974. Contribution of cross-
    cultural friendship to minority group achievement in
    desegregated classrooms. *Sociometry*, pp. 79-91.
Morrison, D. F. 1976. *Multivariate Statistical Methods*.
    New York: McGraw-Hill.
Naylor, H. 1980. Reading disability and lateral asym-
    metry: An information-processing analysis. *Psycho-
    logical Bulletin*, pp. 531-45.
Stanley, G., and R. Hall. 1973. Short-term visual infor-
    mation processing in dyslexics. *Child Development*,
    pp. 841-44.
Stern, G. G. 1970. *People in Context*. New York: Wiley.

5

Data Exploitation and Exploration

In any analysis of Data Exploitation and Exploration:
Mistakes and Techniques (DEMS), the following conclusions
of E. E. Cureton (1950) in his article "Validity, Reliability and Baloney" are relevant:

> When a validity coefficient is computed from
> the same data used in making an item analysis,
> this coefficient cannot be interpreted uncriti-
> cally. And, contrary to many statements in the
> literature, it cannot be interpreted "with cau-
> tion" either. There is one clear interpretation
> for all such validity coefficients. This inter-
> pretation is--"Baloney!"

Those who read this article today might be impressed
with the naivete of the researchers of that decade who
needed to be told not to do such a stupid thing. This im-
pression is correct, but what is not done today is to make
this mistake in such a simple context. We continue to
make this kind of mistake, but in more complicated contexts.

Today, in contrast with the fifties, we distinguish
between data exploration (Tukey 1977) and data exploitation. For awhile there seemed to be some confusion. Researchers held that data should not be looked at but
should be blindly analyzed. This attitude no longer prevails, but sometimes there is a fine line between the two.
I am sure not all readers will agree with where I draw
that line in some cases, but I will attempt to draw it. I
will draw it in the contexts of multiple regression, multimethod-multitrait matrices, and factor analysis. Some

statistical issues that come up in the context of the analysis of variance will be discussed, but it is apparent
that experimentally oriented researchers do not commit
DEMS.   They are more likely to fail to explore their data
and eventually admonitions by Tukey (1977) will permeate
to that group of people.

MULTIPLE REGRESSION
      The item analysis procedure discussed by Cureton
(1950) parallels the multiple regression procedure. The
difference is that the former uses only 0 or 1 weights and
items are selected or rejected, whereas the latter results
in weights that may take on any value. What we see very
often in today's research, particularly in the analysis of
surveys (e.g., Bayer and Astin 1975), is the use of stepwise procedures. Tables are presented that include multiple correlations and significance levels at each step.
These indices are conceptually identical to the validity
coefficient that Cureton labels baloney.
      If one had thousands of observations and only a few
independent variables, little risk would be involved in
searching for a reduced model. But even with thousands of
cases, if one selects only a few variables from many--es-
pecially when the last few variables selected account for
small proportions of variance--the biases in these indices
are relatively large, the multiple correlations are too
big, and the significance levels are too small.
      As has been previously noted (Wolins 1967), these
stepwise procedures serve to identify the most promising
subsets of variables to use in a cross-validation study
and as such constitute data exploration techniques. But
when one reports significance tests, multiple correlations, and the biased regression coefficients, one has
crossed the line to exploitation, not exploration.
      In the context of the well-known bias in conditional
tests and the bias in the associated estimates (Bock et
al., 1973), a Monte Carlo study of the efficacy of the
various stepwise procedures (McCornack 1970) is disap-
pointing. McCornack based the evaluation of these procedures on how well the weights derived from the stepwise
procedure performed when used in a cross-validation sample. However, a legitimate use is to decide on what variables to use rather than how to weight them. Thus in some
sense this study should have reported for each procedure
the extent to which the best variables were selected

disregarding the biased estimates. That is, he should
have asked, How well would the variables selected perform
when properly weighted? I find less interest in how im-
properly weighted variables perform since I would not usually use the regression weights derived from a stepwise
procedure on a cross-validation sample. I would use the
weights derived from the cross-validation sample since
these weights are unbiased.

A further problem with this study is that the efficacy of each procedure was evaluated on how well the biased
weights worked on a cross-validation sample. Why draw a
sample when the population covariance matrix is available?
To evaluate a regression model on the basis of a sample
when the population is available, as it always is in Monte
Carlo studies, results in unnecessary random variability.

Finally, in this context, McCornack does not recognize a pervasive problem of the social sciences--measure-
ment error. In inverting a matrix, measurement error ac-
cumulates and contributes to the error of each coefficient. As a result one should try to keep the matrix that
is to be inverted as small as possible. For this reason
the forward procedure is preferred to the backward procedure. Of course the best procedure is all possible combinations because it is completely exploitive. But even
with modern computers this may be prohibitively expensive
with large numbers of independent variables.

HYPOTHESIS TESTING, ESTIMATION, AND TRANSFORMATIONS

The researcher should regard the question of statistical significance as a separate problem from estimation.
For example, in working with some insurance companies,
data were collected on the claim cost for accidents for
many drivers. The distribution of cost in dollars was
very skewed. A square-root transformation was effective
in several ways. However, the representatives of the insurance companies were quick to point out that they do not
pay claims in units of $\sqrt{\$}$.

Many problems arose. For example, means on the original scale were not close to the square of the means on
the transformed scale. That is, $[E(X)]^2 \neq E(X^2)$. Because of the many extreme scores, relationships with the
cost measures were highly dependent on which scale was
used. Many more significant correlations, meaningless and
not reproducible, occurred when the dollar scale was used.
On the other hand, the small but significant relationships

found using the transformed scale did hold up across companies and over time. The solution was to screen the data with parametric hypothesis testing techniques using the transformed scale and report the results of these analyses using the original scale. Management was shown actual distributions, means, medians, and interquartile ranges.

In my opinion, this is the proper procedure. What a transformation can do is place the nonrandom element in the data into a single parameter such as a mean or a correlation. When the transformation accomplishes this, one need not give the same degree of attention to other aspects of the data such as skewness and nonlinearity. The results can be absorbed and communicated better when the results are compact. After arriving at this compact summary and deciding what needs to be communicated, the problem of expressing the results occurs. The significance tests served to screen the data--to separate the gold from the sand--and, with the transformed scale, the holes in the screen are uniform in size. On the original scale some holes are bigger than others. After screening, nuggets can be evaluated according to whatever criteria seem appropriate.

There are risks involved in transforming data even when there is no concern about estimation. For example, if one were to explore a variety of transformations to find out which one of them results in most nearly meeting some parametric assumptions, the test is biased. This kind of data exploration-exploitation may be reasonable when properly labeled but is wrong when not properly labeled. However, acquaintance with the literature suggests that this kind of exploration does not occur enough. Researchers are reluctant to transform data and their reasons seem vague or are blatantly incorrect.

Because the social and behavioral scientist is frequently required to analyze ad hoc scales or well-developed scales using new populations, he should almost always look at the data prior to analysis to find out if a transformation will provide a reasonable basis for compact analysis.

MULTIMETHOD-MULTITRAIT MATRICES (MMMT)

Campbell and Fiske (1959) defined a design and a way of looking at an important measurement problem. They recognized that a particular measure may not measure its intended construct but may measure other than the intended

one or be a measure of a method more so than a trait
(e.g., ability to get good scores on multiple-choice
tests). Ideally they would ask that one method of measuring a particular trait should correlate highly with other
methods of measuring that trait but correlate lowly with
measures of other traits. As has been stated in each of
the previous chapters, data must be looked at before analysis to judge what method of analysis might be appropriate. Inherent in this statement is the notion that Campbell and Fiske did not propose a method of analysis, as I
have used the term, but a way of looking at data. Others
have proposed methods of analysis (Boruch and Wolins 1970,
Jöreskog 1971, Kavanaugh et al. 1971) and these methods
have produced some confusion. This section is an attempt
to resolve some of that confusion.

The methods of analysis of MMMT matrices are related
to both analysis of variance and factor analysis. In order to confront the first problem in the most straight
forward manner, I will start with the analysis of variance
in an agricultural context and latter address the problem
in the more complicated social science context within the
factor analysis framework.

Consider the researcher in agriculture who has three
kinds of herbicides and three kinds of pesticides that he
wishes to evaluate in terms of their effect on yield,
bushels of corn per acre. Also, suppose he is concerned
with interaction effects--that the combination of pesticide and herbicide might influence yield--so that he
wishes to explore all nine combinations of these two kinds
of treatments. To do this he randomly selects 100 farms
from some large population of farms and performs the experiment. The conventional analysis of such data in agriculture and practically all other areas except the social
sciences is based on the following model,

$$Y_{ijk} = \mu + A_i + B_j + C_k + (AB)_{ij} + e_{ijk}, \quad C_k \sim NID(0, \sigma_C^2)$$

and Table 5.1.

This model assumes that blocks do not interact with
treatments so if a farmer asked the researcher, How does
my farm compare with the other farms that you used in this
study? the researcher could look at σ_C^2 or $\sigma_C^2/(\sigma_C^2 + \sigma_e^2/9)$
to evaluate the reliability of the measurement and report
to the farmer with a clear conscience the point estimate
with a confidence interval. The reader should note that

Table 5.1. The analysis of variance of a three-way factorial
with random blocks--no interaction with blocks

Source	df	EMS
A	2	$\sigma_e^2 + 300\kappa_A^2$
B	2	$\sigma_e^2 + 300\kappa_B^2$
AB	4	$\sigma_e^2 + 100\kappa_{AB}^2$
C	99	$\sigma_e^2 + 9\sigma_C^2$
e	(8)(99)	σ_e^2

each nondiagonal entry in the covariance matrix among the
nine treatments has expectation of σ_C^2 and the diagonal
entrees in that matrix are expected to be $\sigma_C^2 + \sigma_e^2$. The
correlations among the 9 measures of the farms are expect-
ed to be $\sigma_C^2/(\sigma_C^2 + \sigma_e^2)$, asymptotically, and the Spearman-
Brown formula gives $\sigma_C^2/(\sigma_C^2 + \sigma_e^2/9)$.

Suppose the researcher is unwilling to assume that
blocks do not interact with treatments. Suppose he knows
that the different farmers used a variety of herbicides
and pesticides the previous years (despite the commercials
we hear on Iowa television stations), and that the various chemicals leave unequal amounts of residues, and that
the infections vary from farm to farm. So this agricultural researcher writes the unusual model,

$$Y_{ijk} = \mu + A_i + (AC)_{ik} + B_j + (BC)_{jk} + (AB)_{ij} + C_k + e_{ijk}$$

$$C \sim NID(0,\sigma_C^2)$$

and Table 5.2. You will find these EMSs reported in most
modern textbooks. Ostle and Mensing (1975, p. 405) have
essentially laid this out. The problem is that the variance component for the random effect is not the same in
the model as in the EMS table. In a sense, statisticians
are inconsistent, but in another sense they are correct.
Let us explore this inconsistency in the context of the
farmers question--a question that most agricultural researchers are not asked and are not concerned with but is
of extreme importance to the social scientist.

Suppose the agricultural researcher assumed this second model and was asked about the relative performance of

Table 5.2. The analysis of variance of a three-way factorial with random blocks--blocks interact with the fixed effects

Source	df	EMS
A	2	$\sigma_e^2 + 3\sigma_{AC}^2 + 300K_A^2$
AC	(2)(99)	$\sigma_e^2 + 3\sigma_{AC}^2$
B	2	$\sigma_e^2 + 3\sigma_{BC}^2 + 300K_B^2$
BC	(2)(99)	$\sigma_e^2 + 3\sigma_{BC}^2$
AB	4	$\sigma_e^2 + 100K_{AB}^2$
C	99	$\sigma_e^2 + 9\sigma_C^2$ *
e	(4)(99)	σ_e^2

*This variance component is not correct.

a farm. How should he answer? Suppose he observed the covariance matrix in Table 5.3.

The researcher might initially respond, "There is no basis for saying one farm is better than another overall. How a farm performs depends on the treatment conditions." So the farmer replies, "Well, tell me how I did for each pesticide and each herbicide." "O K," the researcher replies, "but the answer won't be very practical since the answer for each pesticide depends on growing one-third of your crop using each herbicide and the same would be true for each herbicide." "That's true," the farmer admits, "It's not practical to use three different chemicals." The farmer then asks, "What *can* you tell me?" The researcher must answer honestly, "Nothing useful."

Table 5.3. Hypothetical covariances among nine treatment conditions

	A_1B_1	A_1B_2	A_1B_3	A_2B_1	A_2B_2	A_2B_3	A_3B_1	A_3B_2	A_3B_3
A_1B_1	10	5	5	5	0	0	5	0	0
A_1B_2		10	5	0	5	0	0	5	0
A_1B_3			10	0	0	5	0	0	5
A_2B_1				10	5	5	5	0	0
A_2B_2					10	5	0	5	0
A_2B_3						10	0	0	5
A_3B_1							10	5	5
A_3B_2								10	5
A_3B_3									10

Suppose we modify these results somewhat. Keep the
quantities of 10 and 5 in the matrix the same but change
the zero values to 3. Now how does the researcher answer
the farmer? He should say, "There is clear evidence from
the data that some farms are better than others, but the
data also indicate that the performance of each farm is
dependent on the particular herbicides and pesticides
used. As a result the only score I can give you reflects
partly the quality of your farm but also reflects how
these particular chemicals influence your farm. With different chemicals your farm might get a considerably higher
or lower score, and the confidence interval I can give you
does not reflect variability due to chemicals other than
these nine. So I can give you a point estimate and a confidence interval. But these statistics depend in part in
the use of all nine of these chemicals on your farm, which
of course is impractical."

The reader should appreciate that this confidence interval is based on the σ_C^2 in the EMS table and not on the
variance of C_k as given in the model. One cannot estimate
the C_k (Schönemann and Wang 1972); yet from the point of
view of the farmer, C_k is what he wants to know about.
All we can give the farmer is

$$\bar{Y}_{..k} = \text{constant} + C_k + \overline{(AC)}_{.k} + \overline{(BC)}_{.k} + \bar{e}_{..k}$$

$$E(S_{\bar{Y}_{..k}}^2) = (\sigma_e^2 + 3\sigma_{AC}^2 + 3\sigma_{BC}^2 + 9\sigma_C^2/9$$

where σ_C^2 is as given in the model but the σ_C^2 in the EMS
table is $\sigma_{AC}^2/3 + \sigma_{BC}^2/3 + \sigma_C^2$.

So the σ_C^2 in the EMS table, which I will relabel as
Σ_C^2, properly goes with $\bar{Y}_{..k}$, which is the only reasonable
way to answer the farmer's question. In this sense the
statistician is correct. He is inconsistent however, and
this mistake got by him probably because conventional ap-
plications attach little importance to σ_C^2. One should al-
so recognize that for finite values of σ_{AC}^2 and σ_{BC}^2, $\bar{Y}_{..k}$
approaches C_k as the number of levels of A and B increase.
So the inconsistency does get smaller in that asymptotic

sense. This is useful to know.

In MMMT matrices a correlation structure that conforms to the above model is sometimes found. For example, Kavanaugh et al. (1971) observed that when department heads were rated by three different sources on many traits, there was not much variability among the coefficients of a particular type (as Campbell and Fiske define type), but the average value from type to type differed considerably. Consequently the analysis of variance approach was a useful data reduction device, reducing hundreds of correlations to four variance components. Kavanaugh et al. (1971) reported Σ^2_C rather than σ^2_C, whereas the latter had been the one attended to by Campbell and Fiske: the hetero-hetero values are the basis of σ^2_C. To the psychologists σ^2_C reflects the squared value of a variable's loading on a general factor, and the notion of a general factor is inherent in the design associated with MMMT matrices. That is, one does not ask if aggression is discriminant from quantitative ability because it is obvious that it is. One asks if aggression is discriminant from dominance or quantitative ability is discriminant from numerical ability. Traits included in an MMMT study are chosen purposely because they are expected to be related. Even when the coefficients of a particular type are not homogeneous, one may expect all the correlations to be positive and possibly all hetero-hetero values may be well fit by a general factor. If one obtained a good fit for these hetero-hetero values by the procedure discussed by Boruch and Wolins (1970) and Jöreskog (1971), the squared loadings on this general factor are analogous to σ^2_C and not Σ^2_C. If the analysis of variance model held, each variable would load the same on this general factor and these squared loadings would be identical to the σ^2_C where $\Sigma^2_C = \sigma^2_{AC}/3 + \sigma^2_{BC}/3 + \sigma^2_C$ as discussed previously. If these loadings are not the same, one may infer this general factor is measured better by some variables than others.

The interpretation of the general factor is approximately analogous to the Campbell and Fiske notion of convergent validity. Trait and method factors precisely conform to the Campbell and Fiske notions of discriminant validity and method bias. Since the latter two conform precisely, it would seem that the notion of a general

factor is a better concept to use than convergent validity
since it conforms better to these analytical techniques.
On the other hand, none of these analytical techniques
seem to fit data very well; so the most valuable way to
approach MMMT matrices seems to be by looking at them.
One probable reason these analytical techniques do not fit
the data very well is that because of the nature of the
problem the measures used are exploratory and are not well
developed psychometric instruments. As a result the distributions are probably messy, the relationships are non-
linear, and the errors within a measure are heterogeneous.
This explanation would be less tenuous if more researchers
would report their inspections of distributions and scatterplots.

Another major problem associated with the factor
analysis approach to MMMT matrices is that we are attempt-
ing to extract much information from data. With three
methods and three traits a simple factor analysis model
would require that we estimate 36 parameters. An important question is, How much data (OUs) do we need to estimate 36 parameters? The answer is both complicated and
ambiguous but I can tell you that I simply have never seen
an MMMT matrix based on enough data. I have analyzed many
such matrices based on 100 or 200 OUs, but I am not con-
vinced the analysis enhanced the understanding of the
data. I suspect the low sample size is part of the reason
for this. I suspect several thousand OUs are necessary
for this refined technique to be more informative than
looking at the matrix and distributions. When data based
on many variables occur, it becomes extremely difficult to
merely look, and the application of one or the other of
these analytical techniques is necessary but would not
stand alone. For example, one might be able to fit subsets of variables or some of the variables well, but not
all of them. Those that are not fit analytically may be
looked at. Thereby one may come away with a reasonably
succinct description of results to be communicated to others. This is sometimes all that can be done and is often
worth doing. One does not deny, however, that such data
exploitation is risky; thus in reporting such results, the
researcher should always offer appropriate admonitions.
But I think the case has been well made that one should
not ignore important information in data just because the
data are messy (Tukey 1977).

In analyzing an MMMT matrix by means of restricted
factor analysis one should always start with a general

factor and a factor for each trait and method, restricting all factors to be orthogonal as suggested by Boruch and Wolins (1970) rather than allowing the method and trait factors to correlate as suggested by Jöreskog (1971). The reason for this is that the general factor approach requires estimating fewer parameters than allowing the method and trait factors to be correlated. The general factor approach requires estimating mt parameters for it whereas allowing the method and trait factors to correlate requires estimating $mt(mt - 1)/2$ parameters. If the general factor approach does not work for one of the several reasons both articles discuss, allowing the factors to correlate is one of a large number of alternatives one may persue in exploring the data. This general factor approach is usually most parsimonious of the reasonable models that recognize the existence of all traits and methods.

Other parsimonious approaches include allowing only the trait factors to be correlated or allowing the correlation of the method factors but restricting the correlation between the two kinds of factors to zero. However, I do not believe these latter approaches are meaningful. Although it makes sense to think of traits being correlated, I cannot get a cognitive grip on the idea of methods being correlated. For me, the hetero-hetero values stem from the measure, the whole measure, and not from the method or trait variance. Thus it makes more sense to allow all $m + t$ factors to correlate and then factor analyze the resulting matrix of oblique correlations. If one factor provides a satisfactory fit to this matrix, one may use Wherry's (1959) procedure to introduce this general factor. If the oblique matrix is factorially complex, one may introduce more than one general factor or attempt to integrate these oblique correlations with the factor loadings in making inferences.

FACTOR ANALYSIS
    There is more folklore attached to factor analysis than to any other statistical procedure that I know about. I attribute this to people seeking simplistic answers to complicated questions. Most of the time the correct answers to such questions depend on properties of particular data sets as well as the purpose of the analysis. A consideration of the correct and incorrect answers to such questions that are related to properties of data sets and the purpose of the analysis follows.

How Large a Sample of Observational Units Do I Need?

The usual incorrect answer is that it depends on the number of variables. For example, one might say you need 30 OUs for each variable. In order to get the researcher "in the right ball park" one must consider three interrelated questions:

1. Do you want to merely identify what factors exist in terms of content or, in addition, is it necessary to obtain good estimates of individual factor loadings?

2. How many factors do you think you will have?

3. Are the variables expected to be normally distributed and highly correlated, as might be expected when they are well developed psychometric instruments, or are the variables short subtests or test items that cannot be highly correlated because of low reliability and nonlinearity?

If the response to the first question indicates that good estimates of factor loadings are essential, an impractically large sample is necessary. Moreover, if the variables are not well behaved, as would be the case in which the variables are items, a large sample would not be the whole answer. With well-behaved variables, each of which has communalities of .5 or higher, perhaps 30 observations per *factor loading* would suffice. If communalities are generally less than .5, perhaps one would need 60 OUs per factor loading.

For example, to obtain 5 factors from 20 variables one must solve 210 equations for 110 unknowns using maximum likelihood. One might draw the analogy here to multiple regression in which one is seeking optimum weights for 110 predictor variables based on 210 OUs. However, the analogy breaks down because, in a sense, the OUs in factor analysis are the correlations rather than people. But the stability of these equations in factor analysis depends on the number of people as well as the communalities, and one must have very stable equations in order to obtain precise solutions to a large number of them. The statistical problem is related to Scheffe's solution in multiple comparisons--there are so many rejection areas in the multivariate confidence interval that huge samples sizes are required to avoid individual factor loadings falling outside of the interval.

Fortunately most investigators use factor analysis to summarize data rather than to obtain precise estimates of factor loadings. For example, they might factor analyze a morale questionnaire in order to verify that items written to measure each specific facet of a work environment load on the same factor. The intention is to take those items that load highly on the factor as the basis of a subtest in which the items are unit weighted to form the subtest scores. The investigator is guided by both the content of the item and the factor loading in his decision to include an item in a subtest or not. Also he should be aware of difficulty factors (Rummel 1970) and use the item difficulties to augment his judgment about whether an item should be included in a subtest or not. Under these circumstances a true factor loading could be .5 and the right decision would be made most of the time if the sample estimate were .3 or .7. Similarly if the true factor loading were zero, the investigator could ignore an occasional +.3 or -.3 because it doesn't make sense in context. As a result, 60 OUs per *factor* would suffice in this case and perhaps 30 OUs per *factor* would suffice for well-behaved variables. These sample sizes would be sufficient for 3 variables or 3000 variables. Of course one needs a sufficient number of variables to identify the relevant factors, but the important idea is that the number of variables is usually not a primary consideration in deciding what the sample size should be. One expects more strange factor loadings from a large matrix than a small one but the proportion of strange loadings should be about the same.

How Many Factors Appear to be Present?

If the purpose of the factor analysis is to estimate factor loadings, one must know the answer to this question before starting the research. If the answer is based on the data, one cannot claim the estimates are unbiased. However, for exploratory or descriptive purposes the answer does not depend on the magnitude of the latent roots--a factor should not be rotated just because the root is greater than one.

A perspective of the problem may be perceived by imagining lumps of information of various sizes in a sea of noise. Or one may consider tuning a radio in which some stations come in clearly, others are barely audible, and still others are overwhelmed by static and are not understandable. One may approach the number-of-factors problem with the intention of identifying the information in the sea of data without attaching spurious interpretations to the static or noise. One should seek out the big lumps and leave the small lumps in the residual table along with the noise.

It is fairly common for investigators to extract too many factors and after rotation to label some of them as residual factors or unexplained. This is usually a poor practice because the noise in the excess factors extracted gets spread over the big factors through rotation (this does *not* pertain to the problem in the maximum-likelihood extraction procedure in which the whole solution is dependent on the number of factors). This is particularly true when the rotation procedure is analytical (e.g., varimax) because the interpretation dictated by the rotated results might be highly dependent on the number of factors extracted. As a result it is recommended that one rotate a range of number of factors and choose the solution that will allow for each factor to be interpreted.

There are exceptions to this. Difficulty factors are often large factors that cannot be interpreted on the basis of content but must be extracted because smaller factors are interpretable on the basis of content. However, if difficulty factors are anticipated, the investigator should be able to identify them by checking to see if the size of the factor loadings on a particular factor is related to the item means or difficulties. At other times, large factors are not interpretable but smaller ones are. This might be a rotation problem. In any case, one is obligated to extract and communicate to the audience this large, uninterpretable factor.

Although the absolute magnitude of the roots are not informative for deciding on the number of factors, their pattern is. Although inspection of the scree (Cattell 1978) is seldom unambiguous in that there are usually either several breaks or there appears to be a smooth decline in the roots with no breaks, it is usually clear from the scree what the maximum number of factors is-- where the curve appears to reach an asymtote. Since rotation is very cheap, one may usually rotate from two to this maximum number. Then one should inspect the largest solution first and work backwards until one finds a satisfactory solution. If one inspects for each solution, the rotated factor with the smallest variance rather than the whole solution, these larger solution may be rejected quickly.

How Should the Factors be Extracted?

The principal components procedure applied to correlation matrices with unities in the diagonal is not a method of factor analysis. Rotating such a solution is foolish. Factor analysis recognizes error and specific variance and is thereby a *statistical* procedure sometimes appropriate for analyzing social science variables. Principal components procedure is a mathematical procedure and only in special contexts is it related to statistics. Its erroneous use as a factor analysis procedure implies that the variables analyzed are error free and no variable has specific variance.

The maximum likelihood procedure is almost always best; yet like many high quality items, the cost is not always worth the benefit. When the number of variables is large, maximum likelihood becomes expensive and existing programs will handle only 80 to 100 variables. But maximum likelihood and least square differ only with respect to the diagonal elements (Harman and Jones 1966). But as the size of the matrix increases, the proportion of matrix elements that are diagonal decreases; with 10 variables 18 percent are diagonal, with 100 variables 2 percent are diagonal. Thus with 100 variables it will usually make little difference what procedure is used as long as the diagonal entries are reasonable (not 1.00s). When extracting relatively few factors from a large matrix (i.e. 10 factors based on 200 variables), I use the largest correlation in the diagonal and extract by least square without iteration. If I had 10 well-behaved variables and expected two or three factors, I would certainly use maximum likelihood. Also if I needed 10 factors from 50 variables I would use maximum likelihood if I could afford it, but iterative least square would be acceptable in this case. When the purpose of the analysis is to estimate factor loadings, maximum likelihood is the only acceptable procedure.

How Should the Factors be Rotated?

There is no wrong way to rotate factors and no one method is generally best. I have preferences and a few recommendations however.

Varimax is a good way to start but it should not always be the end result. By perusing a varimax solution one may get a good idea of the best way to portray the results through rotation. For example, one may note that positive manifold exists and one may choose to rotate in

general factors as suggested by Wherry (1959). In another
situation certain of the variables are of special interest
and the choice is made of one or more of these as targets
and a reference vector is placed through one more of these
through a procedure called Procrustes. Rotating intuitively using graphical procedures is a good way to get
familiar with the data and is not arduous with computer
assistance.

I am biased against oblique procedures because the
factor loadings seem "too big"--they do not reproduce the
correlation matrix in any simple way. Big loadings can
result from small variations in the correlations. Also
the angular cosines and the factors must be inspected at
the same time in order to understand the whole picture and
that boggles the mind. Although oblique rotation is by no
means incorrect, the complexity of basing inferences on
two interrelated matrices leads to mistakes in inferences.
These angular cosines are commonly ignored even when their
structure is interesting. Similarly, investigators frequently ignore the existence of positive manifold in an
orthogonal rotation and thereby do not place in proper
perspective higher-order factors. Such rotations may result in each variable loading positively everywhere but
higher on certain factors than others. A simplistic example is a 50 variable, five factor example in which each
of five sets of 10 variables load .5 on one of the five
factors and .1 on each of the four remaining ones. This
orthogonal rotation invites one to interpret the five factors but ignore that subtests composed of these five sets
of 10 items would correlate about .36. If one introduced
a general factor by means of Wherry's (1959) procedure,
one would observe that each variable loads about .36 on
the general factor and about .40 on its group factor. The
correlation matrix seems to be better described by this
representation than by representations based on either oblique rotation or the conventional orthogonal one.

Wherry's Rotation Procedure

Wherry (1959) couched his rotation procedure in the
context of multiple-group factor analysis, a factor extraction procedure that was reasonable prior to modern al-
gorithms. As a result, the algebra involves the correlation matrix R_{nn}, minus the specific variance, ψ_{nn}, rather
than the orthogonal factor matrix, F_{nm}. However,

$$FF' \sim R - \psi$$

so that, with some little difficulty, one may translate Wherry's algebra in such a way that F, rather than R, is manipulated. The procedure is as follows:

Step 1: As with Procrustes rotation, an S_{nm} matrix is defined. Each row of S contains at most, one nonzero number. Each column must contain at least one nonzero number. The nonzero number is either $+1$ or -1 depending on the direction of the loading of the item on the factor which the particular item defines.

For each column of S an inspection of the item content and the profile of factor loadings of each item determines where to place the nonzero elements. The nonzero elements in a column of S define a set of items similar in content that are located close to each other in the hypersphere. An effort should be made to select such sets of items whose average profiles are distinctly different from each other. Otherwise the angular cosines will be very large and will cause problems later in the analysis.

Step 2: $L_{mm} = S'_{mn} F_{nm}$. If any row of L is normalized, there will be a point on the surface of the hypersphere defined by the vector going through the origin and the cluster of items defined by the nonzero elements. However, that procedure can wait until later.

Step 3: Compute LL', which is analogous to the covariances among the disattenuated variables defined by the linear combinations of the items.

Step 4: Form a diagonal matrix from the trace elements of LL' and

$$D = \mathrm{tr}(LL')^{-\frac{1}{2}}$$

Step 5: $\theta = DLL'D$, which contains the angular cosines or correlations among the disattenuated variables.

Step 6: Factor analyze θ to get G_{ma}. Also obtain the residual matrix.

$$E_{mm} = \theta - GG'$$

There is no reason for using maximum likelihood to factor analyze θ. Iterative least square is better for this matrix. These correlations are not distributed as assumed by maximum likelihood; when maximum likelihood is used the communality plus the specific do not add to unity, which is necessary for this rotation procedure.

Step 7: Decompose E using Cholesky's procedure and obtain a B matrix such that

$$BB' = E$$

which is usually lower triangular. However, one may be uncomfortable with a few large residuals in E. Packaged programs allow one to specify the order of decomposition so that one may control which one of the group factors small loadings from items defining another factor will fall.

Step 8: Augment G with B and compute

$$W_{m(a+m)} = \theta^{-1}_{mm} [G|B]_{m(a+m)}$$

Step 9: $T_{m(a+m)} = (DL)'W$

Step 10: $H_{n(a+m)} = F_{nxm}T$, which is the rotated solution.

Now you can look at each row of H and can tell how well each item measures each factor. Here, as for any good rotation procedure, neither the residuals nor the communalities change since TT' is an identity matrix.

SUMMARY

In a sense, DEMs are the opposite of PSAPs, but not because DEMs involve extracting too much information from data and PSAPs too little. DEMs involve pretending biased estimates are unbiased. It is not wrong to argue that independent variable such and such is potentially important in connection with the dependent one on the basis of its early entry into a stepwise procedure or to argue that variable so-and-so is a good measure of a particular construct because it loads highly and meaningfully on a particular factor. But to attach significance levels or confidence intervals to biased estimates degrades the meaning of such statistics when they are used in their proper contexts and is misleading in the context in which they are used.

Data should be explored and if bias in estimation of parameters results from such exploration, that is merely regretable when properly labeled. If incorrectly labeled, it is often misleading and results in unnecessary confusion and controversy.

REFERENCES

Bayer, A. E., and H. S. Astin. 1975. Sex differentials in the academic reward system. *Science*, pp. 796-802.

Bock, M. E., T. A. Yancey, and G. G. Judge. 1973. The statistical consequences of preliminary test estimators in regression. *Journal of the American Statistical Association*, 109-16.

Boruch, R. F., and L. Wolins. 1970. A procedure for estimation of trait, method and error variance attributable to a measure. *Educational and Psychological Measurement*, pp. 547-74.

Campbell, D. T., and Fiske, D. W. 1959. Convergent and discriminant validation by the multitrait-multimethod matrix. *Psychological Bulletin*, pp. 81-105.

Cattell, R. B. 1978. *The Scientific Use of Factor Analysis in Behavioral and Life Sciences*. New York: Plenum Press.

Cureton, E. E. 1950. Validity, reliability and baloney. *Educational and Psychological Measurement*, pp. 94-96.

Harman, H. H., and W. H. Jones. 1966. Factor analysis by minimizing residuals (MINRES). *Psychometrika*, pp. 351-68.

Jöreskog, K. G. 1971. Statistical analysis of sets of congeneric tests. *Psychometrika*, pp. 109-33.

Kavanaugh, M. J., A. C. MacKinney, and L. Wolins. 1971. Issues in managerial performance: Multitrait-multimethod analyses of ratings. *Psychological Bulletin*, pp. 34-49.

McCornack, R. L. 1970. A comparison of three predictor selection techniques in multiple regression. *Psychometrika*, pp. 257-71.

Ostle, B., and R. W. Mensing. 1975. *Statistics in Research*. 3d ed. Ames: Iowa State University Press.

Rummel, R. J. 1970. *Applied Factor Analysis*. Evanston, Ill.: Northwestern University Press.

Schönemann, P. H., and Ming-Mei Wang. 1972. Some new results on factor indeterminacy. *Psychometrika*, pp. 61-91.

Tukey, J. W. 1977. *Exploratory Data Analysis*. Reading,
    Mass.: Addison-Wesley.
Wherry, R. J. 1959. Hierarchical factor solutions with-
    out rotation. *Psychometrika*, pp. 45-51.
Wolins, L. 1967. The use of multiple regression proce-
    dures when the predictor variables are psychological
    tests. *Educational and Psychological Measurement*,
    pp. 821-27.

6

Instrument Development

To some extent this chapter represents an idiosyncratic culmination. If there is a secondary thread holding the first five chapters together, that thread must be labeled measurement problems. The primary focus of the previous chapters has been on recognizing measurement problems in our analyses rather than in overcoming them. In this chapter an attempt will be made to define some measurement problems more clearly, suggest techniques for developing better instruments, and offer reasons for idiosyncratic procedures for the development of instruments.

To start, look at some of the implications of the indeterminancy problem that are discussed in Chapter 5. Suppose we did an experiment to evaluate the impact of Head Start on the children's scores on the Wechsler Intelligence Scale for Children (WISC) of the two different racial groups, black and white. In this dependent variable we must recognize prior research (Reschly 1978) indicating that it is a composite of three conceptual variables: General Intelligence, Performance and Verbal. For simplicity, it is assumed that the black and white populations are reasonably comparable because all children were selected from similar neighborhoods and come from similar socioeconomic levels. Otherwise one could not interpret the interaction between race and treatment. One should use a pretest or covariates obtained prior to treatment but these sources will be neglected for the sake of simplicity. In order to focus on the indeterminacy problem, it is also assumed that the covariances among the subtests are the same for each of the four groups and that this covariance structure conforms to an analysis of variance model in Table 6.1.

Table 6.1. Pooled within-group covariances and the factor loadings three performance (P) and three verbal (V) measures (M) (fictitious results)

	Covariances						Factor Loadings		
	P_1	P_2	P_3	V_1	V_2	V_3	G	P	V
P_1	100	50	50	25	25	25	5	5	0
P_2		100	50	25	25	25	5	5	0
P_3			100	25	25	25	5	5	0
V_1				100	50	50	5	0	5
V_2					100	50	5	0	5
V_3						100	5	0	5

From these results we may immediately estimate the variance components for the random effects: σ^2_{MC} and σ^2_C (not Σ^2_C). These are each 25 in this simplistic example and σ^2_e is 50. We do not deal with these subtests when the dependent variable is IQ so that the within-group variance is 275, the sum of the elements in the 6 × 6 matrix divided by 6. Conceptually this sum is

$$\sigma^2_e + 6\sigma^2_C + 3\sigma^2_{MC}$$

and is the error term for the experiment-investigation. This equation tells us that 18 percent of this total variance is error variance, giving us a reliability of .82. But this 82 percent true variance is 55 percent general and 27 percent specific to the measures. Chapter 5 focuses on the importance of knowing that the indeterminancy problem decreases as the number of different subtests increase. Consequently the ambiguity of scores on such tests as the Wechsler would decrease if the number of different subtests were larger and if the items were selected on the basis of general factor loadings rather than on the basis of internal consistency of the subtests.

Of the many possible nonnull outcomes, we might find that blacks are relatively high in V but not P or G, because of the treatment, and whites improve only on G. Further, if the improvement of the whites on each of the subtests because of G were of the same magnitude as the improvement of blacks on V, it would appear that whites improve on IQ because of the treatment, more than the blacks do. The reason is that there are more subtests

that measure G than there are subtests that measure V, and
the G measurement is thereby more reliable.

The moral to this story is that if a test is heterogeneous in content, inferences based on use of the test
are ambiguous. It is even possible, although unlikely,
that such a dependent variable could result in apparent
null results because the groups increased on one factor
and decreased on another. In this case we know the composite is heterogeneous and a multivariate analytical approach is obviously correct. In this case the preference
would be to code the two main effects and the interaction
using dummy variables and to attach these three variables
to the factors derived from the six dependent ones by
means of Dwyer's extension (1937). This procedure does
not completely solve the indeterminancy problem. For example, if each child improved on both P and V, it may appear that they improved on G. However, if the improvement
is more for some subtests than others, one is likely to
some extent to attribute the improvement to the correct
source.

The pleas for homogeneous subtests and criticisms of
them are discussed in many textbooks in measurement and
factor analysis. These same textbooks either do not discuss factor analysis of test items or merely point out
that the procedure is dangerous because of difficulty factors. Although there is no reason to discuss these clas-
sic problems here, it is essential to mention them because
they intrude into modern psychometrics. Bejar (1980)
makes an urgent and appropriate plea to use scores derived
from latent-trait theory (Lord and Novick 1968) rather
than the classical theory as the basis for evaluation research. The reason for this plea in this book is that
SDMs would be less prevalent. Latent-trait theory assumes
local independence (Lord and Novick 1968), which is latent-trait theory's way of talking about homogeneity. Yet
latent-trait theory offers us nothing for evaluating homogeneity or the procedures for obtaining it.

Both theories offers us item-analysis techniques such
as item-total correlations or the slope parameters, but
these procedures are obviously not sufficient. For example, if the six subtests discussed previously had the same
number of items, the average correlation of each subtests
items with the total, or the average of the slope parameters, would be the same and positive. This would be
true even when no general factor existed. Thus it seems
that homogeneity in some cases is at least desireable,

and despite the problems with factor analysis, no alternatives exist. Thus it is appropriate to consider how these
difficulty factor problems may be surmounted.

FACTOR ANALYSIS OF COGNITIVE ITEMS
    The proper coefficient to use is the phi coefficient
and not the tetrachoric or phi/phimax. The reason is that
the correlation among tests is a simple function of the
phi coefficient and item difficulties but not a simple
function of the other coefficients. If one wishes to ex-
press hierarchical factors from different levels of the
heirarchy on the same scale, one must use these Pearson-
product-moment correlations throughout. For example, if
one factor analyzed an arithmetic test, one might obtain
an addition-subtraction factor, a multiplication-division
factor, and a decimal-ratio factor. If we gave an algebra
and geometry test in addition, we might obtain a general
quantitive factor. If other tests were included, this
quantitative factor would be distinct from, say, a verbal
factor. A factor analysis of the scores derived from subtests that in turn are derived from items loading on the
factors would result in identical solutions, except for a
scalar, to the solutions obtained from the factor analysis
of the angular cosines derived from an oblique rotation of
the factors obtained from the items.
    Unfortunately, phi coefficients are notorious in that
large difficulty factors occur and obscure and contaminate
results. The solution to this problem stems from the fact
that when items are factor analyzed, there are many of
them. In this situation one can afford to lose some. The
recommended procedure is to restrict the common-factor
space to items of moderate difficulty and to use Dwyer's
extension for items of extreme difficulty. This procedure may be complemented by combining two or more items
which are obviously similar in content into a composite
and dichotomizing this composite as close to the median as
possible to produce one item of moderate difficulty. If
one uses these procedures, the difficulty factors will be
small and will probably be lost in the sea of noise.
    When these procedures are used, one should recognize
that the size of the factor loadings still depends on the
item difficulties so that items of extreme difficulty will
necessarily have low communalities. Thus a low communality does not necessarily mean the item is bad--it may mean
instead that it is difficult or easy. One may get a good

feel for how to evaluate an item by plotting the communalities against the item difficulties.

A risk involved in this procedure is that there may
be factors present in easy or difficult items that are not
present in items of moderate difficulty. I do not feel
this risk is large in most cases. But if this were true
in some case, the loss resulting from the procedure would
be small since there was little information regarding such
factors in this data. However, if the sample size were
very large, one might explore this possibility by dividing
the sample into groups on the basis of some other variable
such as socioeconomic status or class rank and then fac-
tor-analyzing groups of items moderate in difficulty for
each group of people.

If the test is generally easy or difficult for the
sample of people, items of moderate difficulty should be
eliminated from the common factor space and the major
analysis should be restricted to easy or difficult items.

The boundaries to use for the item difficulties for
the major analysis depends on the distribution of the item
difficulties, the sample size, and the number of items. I
would feel comfortable if I could restrict the item difficulties to be between .3 and .7 and retain 75 percent of
the items for the major analysis. If I had to go lower
than .2 or higher than .8 in order to retain 75 percent of
the items, I would attempt to combine items judgmentally.
If neither of these procedures worked but the sample size
was large, I would divide the sample and do several factor
analyses as previously discussed. In all probability
there would be some common items to anchor the separate
analyses. If none of these procedures work, either collect more data or do something else. It is not profitable
to factor-analyze items heterogeneous in difficulty. If
the situation becomes desperate, use tetrachorics.

A special problem occurs for such tests as the Stanford-Binet and the Wechsler. The items in the test are
spiraled in difficulty and, using a set of reasonable
rules, all items are not administered to all subjects.
For example, for the Stanford-Binet if preliminary examination of an examinee indicates he is not intelligent, the
examiner may start the examinee with easier items than another examinee who superfically appears bright. An examinee is not presented the easy items if he answers a group
of difficult ones correctly. Similarly, if the examinee
answers incorrectly a group of items homogeneous in difficulty, he is not asked more difficult ones.

The procedure, though practical, interferes with proper analysis. It is evident (Ross-Reynolds 1980) that this procedure leads to biased estimates of item difficulties. If one plots item difficulties for third-grade children against difficulties for the same items for fifth-grade children, one can observe a jog in the function relating the two variables that results from where the examiner typically starts the examination for the two groups. It does happen that an examinee will miss an easy item even though he has answered more difficult ones correctly, or he may answer correctly a difficult item even though he missed an easier one. This information is highly relevant for determining homogeneity and should be recognized procedurally. It is recommended that standard procedures be dropped when the purpose of the data collection is item analysis. Rather, each child should be administered items with a substantially wider range of difficulty.

FACTOR ANALYSIS OF AFFECTIVE ITEMS

Difficulty factors again provide the basis for *not* factor analyzing the items in personality and attitude questionnaires. Although such factor analyses are more common for affective items than cognitive ones since the format for the former is commonly a 5-point rather than a 2-point scale, the 5-point scale still may result in strong difficulty factors. The reason is that the skewness of the response distributions depends on the mean response, and two such response distributions with different skewness are necessarily curvilinearly related if they are positively related.

A procedure for reducing variability due to curvilinearity for attitude items is analogous to the procedure for cognitive tests. For example, one might exclude those items whose means are below 2.00 and above 4.00 from the common factor space, or if the means are generally high, one might exclude items with means lower than 2.5 and above 4.25. However, for affective items a better procedure is to use a 99-point scale and a probit transformation of these responses (Wolins and Dickinson 1973). Subsequent research indicates the 99-point scale procedure has no apparent advantage over the use of the Likert format when scores based on many items are analyzed but offers considerable advantage when short scales or individual items are analyzed. For example, Hendricks (1975) did

an experiment. He sent out about 1500 morale surveys to
Iowa State University employees. Half of the employees
were asked for responses on a 3-point scale and the other
half were asked for responses on a 99-point scale. The
percentage of returns where almost identical for the two
groups and about the same percentage of complete, useable
questionnaires were obtained for each group. Separate
factor analyses were done for each group and the results
clearly indicated that high factor loadings were higher
and low factor loadings were lower with the 99-point scale
than with the 3-point scale and that the associated transformation results in clear and interpretable factors and
should be used to group items into homogeneous scales.
Once they are in groups the 5- or even 3-point scale is
sufficient and from that stage latent-trait analysis is
the procedure recommended and is consistent with the recommendations of Bejar (1980). As was the case with the
Wechsler tests, the procedure recommended for item analysis is not the same as that for the actual use of the
test. But research by Hendricks (1975) indicates the same
factors are obtained by both procedures. This implies
that using a different procedure for grouping items than
for measuring people may be worth the risk.

GROUP DIFFERENCES AND INDIVIDUAL DIFFERENCES
     To illustrate this problem, consider a battery of
achievement tests administered in many elementary schools.
We may focus on the arithmetic test whose content is heterogeneous in that there are several problem types. These
problem types have been decided upon by a group of educational experts. They have judged that these types are
typically covered in classrooms and textbooks used in elementary schools. However, these experts are seldom unani-
mous about the appropriateness of a particular type. In
committee they achieve a compromise by discussing and ar-
guing about how extensively and intensively problems of a
particular type are taught. It is well known that standardized achievement tests are less appropriate than
teacher-made tests in content for the students in a particular school system.
     As a result of this, responses to the items in a
standardized test depend partly on individual differences
and partly on those group differences produced by diversi-
ty in educational experiences. If one factor analyzes
correlations based on all students, the factors that

emerge may not be meaningful because these two sources are confounded. One should factor analyze the pooled-within group correlations. If the number of schools is large, the properly transformed item difficulties ($sin^{-1}\sqrt{p}$) should be factor analyzed using the school as the observational unit. If only a few schools are involved, scatter-plots are informative for identifying items that differ by school

Obviously the factor analysis of the *transformed* item difficulties will not result in the same scale as the factor analysis of the items. Thus the comparison of the between and within is sacrificed. Under null conditions (no group differences) the between-factor loadings should be bigger because the model fits better; for the same reason, difficulty factors should be less prevalent for the between analysis. The latter is the reason for using the transformation, but factor analysis of the untransformed item difficulties also may be informative.

The procedure of pooling covariances for different groups is risky since it sometimes happens that the covariance structure varies from group to group. This was illustrated by Wherry (1954) in his reanalysis of studies by others. When the variables are items responded to according to conventional formats, the covariance structures will necessarily be different from group to group if the groups differ on the factors. That is, the difficulty factors will be different. This problem should be reduced by using the properly transformed responses to the 99-point scale. Yet it often happens that the groups are too small to evaluate whether the covariance structures are the same. Even when each sample size is large, it is difficult to judge whether the apparent differences between the covariances are interpretable or a function of dissimilar difficulty factors emerging through group differences. It is recommended that pooling is desirable despite this reservation. When the samples for the groups are small, the information lost is small since there was little information regarding differences among groups in covariance structures in the first place. On the other hand, the factor analysis of the pooled matrix should be meaningful to the extent that the covariance structures from different groups are similar. When the sample sizes for the groups are large, the mean and variance of composite scores derived from the factor analysis of the pooled matrix will reflect much of the between-group differences in covariance structures, and comparing these two indices is obviously more tractable than comparing covariance structures. When the sample sizes are large, a separate factor analysis for each group could be done and a judgment should be made on whether the information provided by these detailed, albeit less reliable, results is worth reporting in addition to the pooled results. In my experience the pooled and between-group results are always informative but the detailed results are seldom informative for cognitive test items. However, they are frequently informative for affective items.

SUMMARY

The *S-O-R* (Stimulus-Organism-Response) paradigm requires that the stimulus be unambiguous. We must know what the stimulus is to understand the response. It is not always possible to achieve homogeneous tests and for purposes of validity (Woodbury and Novick 1968, Levine 1958) it is not always desirable. When the purpose of research is directed at understanding the impact of a treatment, time invested in the development of homogeneous scales is well spent.

One should regard difficulty factors as a shortcoming of our measurement procedures and not a shortcoming of factor analysis. A limitation of factor analysis is the assumption of linearity and we should direct our attention toward achieving linearity rather than rejecting the only viable procedure for obtaining homogeneous scales. Factor analysis of items cannot be a mechanical procedure—it requires careful planning and good judgment. A mechanical approach to any research problem is risky but the risk is greater for factor analysis, in my opinion.

Individual differences must be analyzed separately from group differences. One might be interested in only one or the other, but it is necessary to recognize both procedurally in order to evaluate one or the other.

Finally, it is a mistake to regard statistics as the private domain of the statistician. Particularly the areas of measurement, statistical methods, and the design of experiments and investigations are inseparably intertwined with the social and behavioral sciences. The quality of research and application in these disciplines is dependent upon how well members of the social and behavioral scientific communities are trained in these statistical areas. As members of the scientific community, individuals serve not only as researchers but also as editors, reviewers, and consumers of research reports. They must be educated in statistics to perform effectively in these roles.

Part of the educational problems in psychology and probably in most of the behavioral and social sciences is that the great majority of psychologists are involved in little or no research and of course are not invited to perform editorial or reviewer roles. I do not know how many are active consumers of research results, but I suspect very few of the nonresearchers actively and critically read the current scientific literature. Thus one may argue that there is little profit in subjecting all students in these areas to education in statistics although this is a point I do not choose to discuss. However, I do not believe that a social or behavioral scientist who aspires to research should be sanctioned by these communities without meeting high standards of achievement in the so-called statistical areas.

Giving this inexorable intertwining of the substance of these sciences with the methods, one must conclude that these statistical areas are best taught by those familiar with both areas. It is clear, as some statisticians (e.g., Federer 1976) have asserted, that social scientists sometimes do an ineffective job of teaching statistics. It is also clear that statisticians sometimes are unsuccessful in teaching certain aspects of statistics to social and behavioral scientists.

REFERENCES

Bejar, I. I. 1980. Biased assessment of program impact due to psychometric artifacts. *Psychological Bulletin*, pp. 513-24.

Dwyer, P. S. 1937. The determination of the factor loadings of a given test from the known factor loadings of other tests. *Psychometrika*, pp. 173-78.

Federer, W. T. 1976. On the teaching of statistics service courses. In Mimeo Series of the Biometrics Unit, Cornell University, Ithaca, N.Y.

Hendricks, R. L. 1975. *The Effects of Response Format and Internal Versus External Criteria Measures on the Evaluation of Importance Weighted Models of Job Satisfaction*. Ph.D. diss., Iowa State University, Ames.

Levine, A. S. 1958. Reflections of a personnel research psychologist. *Personnel Psychology*, pp. 161-78.

Lord, F. M., and M. R. Novick. 1968. *Statistical Theories of Mental Test Scores*. Reading, Mass.: Addison-Wesley.

Reschly, D. J. 1978. WISC-R factor structures among anglos, blacks, chicanos and native-American papagos. *Journal of Consulting Psychology*, pp. 417-22.

Ross-Reynolds, Jane. 1980. *Examination of item bias on the WISC-R for four sociocultural groups*. Master's thesis, Iowa State University, Ames.

Wherry, R. J. 1954. An orthogonal re-rotation of the Baehr and Ash studies of the SRA employee inventory. *Personnel Psychology*, pp. 365-80.

------. 1959. Hierarchical factor solutions without rotation. *Psychometrica*, pp. 45-51.

Wolins, L., and T. L. Dickinson. 1973. Transformations to improve reliability and/or validity for affective scales. *Educational and Psychological Measurement*, pp. 711-13.

Woodbury, M. A., and M. R. Novick. 1968. Maximizing the validity of a test battery as a function of relative test lengths for a fixed total testing time. *Journal of Mathematical Psychology*, pp. 242-59.

I N D E X